Education, Mobilities and Migration

Within the context of increased global migration and mobility, education occupies a central role which is being transformed by new human movements and cultural diversity, flows and networks. Studies under the umbrella terms of migration, mobility and mobilities reveal the complexity of these concepts. The field of study ranges from global child mobility as a response to poverty, to the reconceptualising of notions of inclusion in relation to pastoralist lifestyles, to the ways in which academic migration and new offshore institutions and transnational diasporas shape the educational experiences of students, families and teachers. At the heart of this new research is a need to explore how identity, integration and social stratification play a role in the story of global migration between and within the Global North and South.

This volume focuses on three major themes: poverty, migration, social mobility and social reproduction; networks of migration within and across national education systems; and thirdly, higher education and international student mobility and the concerns and opportunities that go along with this mobility. The international group of researchers who have contributed to this book demonstrate how educational institutions are part of a common global project characterised by fluidity, how the social fabric of educational institutions responds to demographic diversity and how new social differentiations occur as a result of human movement. By bringing these contributions together, a number of important theoretical and empirical methodological dimensions are identified, which need more attention within the growing field of migration and education studies. This volume shows how mobilities and transnational interconnectedness create multiple interactions that tie our different educational projects together. This book was originally published as a special issue of *Compare: A Journal of Comparative and International Education*.

Madeleine Arnot is Professor of Sociology of Education and a Fellow of Jesus College at Cambridge University, UK. She is a co-founder of the Cambridge Migration Research Network and co-author of *Education, Asylum and the Non-Citizen Child: The Politics of Compassion and Belonging* (with Halleli Pinson and Mano Candappa, 2010), which draws upon moral philosophy to explore government and local responses and refugee/asylum-seeking children's school experiences in the United Kingdom. Her recent research focuses on home-school communication and social integration of Eastern European children in the United Kingdom and on the tense relationships between moralities and mobilities.

Claudia Schneider is Principal Lecturer in Social Policy at Anglia Ruskin University, Cambridge, UK. She has researched a wide range of migration areas including German asylum policy, the migration of European citizens from Eastern Europe and international migration in higher education. She has led a number of externally funded projects on Eastern European migration and is currently co-convening a Bell Foundation-funded project with Cambridge University on the social, linguistic and educational needs of pupils who have English as an additional language. Her recent research applies theories of transnationalisation and the role of communication systems to education and migration studies.

Oakleigh Welply is a Lecturer in the School of Education at Durham University, UK. Her research adopts a cross-national perspective in order to investigate the experiences and identities of immigrant-background children in primary schools in France and England. She has a particular interest in developing cross-national theory and methodologies to conduct research with diverse communities in European countries and to explore the relationship of education to issues of language, religion, immigration and citizenship. Using the work of Paul Ricoeur and Pierre Bourdieu, she investigates the notion of 'Otherness' in young people's school experience and how it shapes identity in multicultural classrooms.

Education, Mobilities and Migration

People, ideas and resources

Edited by
**Madeleine Arnot, Claudia Schneider and
Oakleigh Welply**

Routledge
Taylor & Francis Group

LONDON AND NEW YORK

First published 2016
by Routledge

2 Park Square, Milton Park, Abingdon, Oxfordshire OX14 4RN
52 Vanderbilt Avenue, New York, NY 10017

Routledge is an imprint of the Taylor & Francis Group, an informa business

First issued in paperback 2020

British Library Cataloguing in Publication Data
A catalogue record for this book is available from the British Library

ISBN 13: 978-1-138-65503-4 (hbk)
ISBN 13: 978-0-367-59689-7 (pbk)

Typeset in TimesNewRomanPS
by diacriTech, Chennai

Publisher's Note
The publisher accepts responsibility for any inconsistencies that may have arisen during the conversion of this book from journal articles to book chapters, namely the possible inclusion of journal terminology.

Disclaimer
Every effort has been made to contact copyright holders for their permission to reprint material in this book. The publishers would be grateful to hear from any copyright holder who is not here acknowledged and will undertake to rectify any errors or omissions in future editions of this book.

Contents

Citation Information

The chapters in this book were originally published in *Compare*, volume 43, issue 5 (September 2013). When citing this material, please use the original page numbering for each article, as follows:

CITATION INFORMATION

Chapter 5
Negotiating differences: cosmopolitan experiences of international doctoral students
Başak Bilecen
Compare, volume 43, issue 5 (September 2013) pp. 667–688

Chapter 6
'Selective cosmopolitans': tutors' and students' experience of offshore higher education in Dubai
Laila Kadiwal and Irfan A. Rind
Compare, volume 43, issue 5 (September 2013) pp. 689–711

For any permission-related enquiries please visit:
http://www.tandfonline.com/page/help/permissions

Notes on Contributors

Florence Aate Andrew is Chairperson of the Southern Sudanese Women Organisation (SSWAN) and Lecturer at the University of Groningen, Groningen, the Netherlands. Florence's research interests include humanitarian development, women's empowerment and capacity building, ethnicity, and migration and development.

Madeleine Arnot is Professor of Sociology of Education, and a Fellow of Jesus College, at Cambridge University, UK. She is a co-founder of the Cambridge Migration Research Network and co-author of *Education, Asylum and the Non-Citizen Child: The Politics of Compassion and Belonging* (with Halleli Pinson and Mano Candappa, 2010), which draws upon moral philosophy to explore government and local responses and refugee/asylum-seeking children's school experiences in the United Kingdom. Her recent research focuses on home-school communication and social integration of Eastern European children in the United Kingdom and on the tense relationships between moralities and mobilities.

Başak Bilecen is a Lecturer and Research Fellow in the Faculty of Sociology at Bielefeld University, Bielefeld, Germany. Her research interests include the sociology of migration, international student mobility and social protection. Başak has contributed numerous articles to her field, which have been published in journals such as *Population, Space and Place* and *Compare: A Journal of International and Comparative Education*. Her first book, *International Student Mobility and Transnational Friendships*, was published in 2014.

Marit Blaak is Lecturer and Education, Training and Research Consultant in the Department of Lifelong Learning, Faculty of Social and Behavioural Sciences, University of Groningen, Groningen, the Netherlands. Her research focuses on adult education and global educational development. Marit teaches undergraduate and graduate courses in various areas of education, including globalisation and lifelong learning, and social and educational intervention. Her publications can be found in the *International Journal of Educational Development* and *Compare: A Journal of International and Comparative Education*.

NOTES ON CONTRIBUTORS

Jo Boyden is Professor of International Development at the University of Oxford, UK. Her research takes a multidisciplinary approach, focusing on child development, childhood poverty and children's rights. Jo is co-author of the recently published *Growing Up in Poverty: Perspectives from Young Lives* (2014) and *Childhood Poverty: Multidisciplinary Approaches* (2012). She is also Director of Young Lives, an international research project recording changes in child poverty.

Caroline Dyer is Professor of Education and International Development at the University of Leeds, UK. Her research interests lie in education, social inclusion and social justice. Caroline teaches courses in education and global development, and is chair of the Editorial Board of the journal *Compare: A Journal of International and Comparative Education*. Her publications include *Livelihoods and Learning: Education for All and the Marginalisation of Mobile Pastoralists* (Routledge, 2014) and *Operation Blackboard: Policy Implementation in Indian Elementary Education* (Routledge, 2000).

Laila Kadiwal is a Research Fellow in Education, Teachers & Peacebuilding in the Department of Education at the University of Sussex, Brighton, UK. Her research focuses on religion, globalisation and international education.

Volodymyr Kulyk is Associate Professor and Leading Research Fellow in Political and Ethnic Studies at the National Academy of Sciences of Ukraine, Kyiv, Ukraine. He has published widely in the areas of Ukrainian politics, media and language. His recent works have appeared in *Europe-Asia Studies*, *National Identities* and *Security and Human Rights*.

Irfan A. Rind is Assistant Professor and Head of the Department of Education Management at the Sukkur Institute of Business Administration, Sukkur, Pakistan. His articles have appeared in journals such as the *International Journal of Lifelong Education* and *Educational Futures*.

Claudia Schneider is Principal Lecturer in Social Policy at Anglia Ruskin University, Cambridge, UK. She has researched a wide range of migration areas including German asylum policy, the migration of European citizens from Eastern Europe and international migration in higher education. She has led a number of externally funded projects on Eastern European migration and is currently co-convening a Bell Foundation-funded project with Cambridge University on the social, linguistic and educational needs of pupils who have English as an additional language. Her recent research applies theories of transnationalisation and the role of communication systems to education and migration studies.

Josje van der Linden is a Lecturer in the Department of Lifelong Learning, Faculty of Social and Behavioural Sciences, University of Groningen, Groningen, the Netherlands. Her research interests include international educational development, non-formal education, professional development and adult education. Josje's publications have appeared in journals such as the *International Journal of Educational Development* and *Adult Education Quarterly*.

Oakleigh Welply is a Lecturer in the School of Education at Durham University, UK. Her research adopts a cross-national perspective in order to investigate the experiences and identities of immigrant-background children in primary schools in France and England. She has a particular interest in developing cross-national theory and methodologies to conduct research with diverse communities in European countries and to explore the relationship of education to issues of language, religion, immigration and citizenship. Using the work of Paul Ricoeur and Pierre Bourdieu, she investigates the notion of 'Otherness' in young people's school experience and how it shapes identity in multicultural classrooms.

INTRODUCTION

Education, mobilities and migration: people, ideas and resources

Within a context of increased globalisation, the fields of migration, mobilities and education have become growing areas of interest in international and comparative education – as evidenced by the number of papers on the topic in *Compare*, including the special issue of March 2010, 'Migration, Education and Socio-Economic Mobility'. The international BAICE conference in September 2012, Education, Mobility and Migration: People, Ideas and Resources, demonstrated the wide variety of perspectives on the issue and raised new questions, both empirical and theoretical, with regard to the educational experiences of different migrant groups and the new challenges these present for educational practice and policies at local, national and global levels.

Education is at the centre of this context of increased migration and mobility (Adams and Kirova 2007). Rethinking the role of education in relation to new movements, flows and networks, and new forms of diversity and identity has become central to educational discourse, in both policy and research. Consequently, there is the need to account for the complexity that lies beneath the umbrella terms 'migration' and 'mobility' or 'mobilities'. Whilst migration usually refers to the movement of people across geographic boundaries to reside in a different country, region or location, mobility is mostly used to refer to the ability to move within a social structure (such as social mobility) or across space (physical mobility) or the ability of knowledge, ideas and practices to move across national educational systems and institutions. Current research has approached these concepts from many different angles and, in practice, they are often used interchangeably since migration of people often involves various forms of social, geographic and educational mobilities. In a demographically mobile age, it is hard to distinguish between these two associated elements. Thus, some focus on the nature of migration patterns within different national contexts, exploring, for example, how migrants are received and how they experience the political, cultural and educational conditions of their new country (Rutter 1999). Migration researchers seek out the experiences of young migrants in school, parents' perceptions and educational beliefs, as well as tapping teachers' views and practice in relation to particular migrant groups, from both a national and a cross-national perspective (for example Pinson, Arnot, and Candappa's [2010] research on refugees and asylum-seeking students). Others examine

1

the processes of acculturation, integration, inclusion, language issues and social identity construction through education (for example Vertovec and Wessendorf 2009; Welply 2010). Alternatively, educationalists critically assess at the policy level how, for example, immigration and asylum policies affect the provision of education for different groups of migrants (for example Demirdjian 2012). The politics of immigration reveals a good deal about the cultural ethos of countries and the expectations that educational institutions can cope with and resolve the tensions such politics create.

Secondly, at the international level, studies on migration and education focus particularly on immigration patterns from the global South to North. Arguably this is the most politically controversial aspect of migration today since this pattern has triggered the aggressively hostile conditions that migrant groups experience in, for example, Europe, the USA and Australasia. Closed-door immigration legislation and citizenship rights reflect the powerful presence of discrimination based on race, ethnicity, xenophobia and Islamophobia in schools and society in the global North. Researchers have drawn attention to the consequences of such international migration and its implications for the global South (e.g. Rao 2010). The financial and economic benefits from migration for the sending countries – such as remittances that help stimulate development, for example, by financing schooling in developing countries – have been recognised but so too have their negative consequences. The effect of this economic analysis is that migration studies in the past focused, first, on:

> ... the investment of migrant remittances in the education of their children back home; and second, the perspective of 'brain drain' that refers to the migration of skilled workers from the developing to the developed world. (Rao 2010, 137)

As Cao (1996) points out, early studies expressed worries about highly skilled professionals moving out of the sending countries and not necessarily returning or being in a position to transfer back skills. However, these flows are not unilateral or uni-dimensional – it is more the case of 'brain circulation'. Recent studies stress the complexity of transnational interconnections between the sending and the receiving countries.

Thirdly, migration also occurs from South to South. Such migration carries its own challenges in relation to education, not least its challenges to simple notions of push/pull dynamics. The majority of the world's migrants have moved from one developing country to another (World Bank 2011). There is considerable danger that, in income-poor countries, migrant communities receive little support and can instead encounter hostile responses and discriminatory practices from those whose livelihoods might be thought to be threatened (see Bartlett 2012).

These three migratory patterns alone do not do justice to the complexity of migration and the transformations that it brings to educational systems, to those who participate in educational institutions and to the pedagogical/ professional practice that is confronted with previously unknown levels of diversity, plurality and difference. Migration changes the social fabric of educational institutions and its purposes by increasing diversity but also by challenging the ways in which they function as learning centres and places of socialisation, and also their methods of dealing with shifting notions of what citizen rights, welfare and employment entitlements are made available to the newly arrived group. The movement of educational ideas, of educational personnel and the migrant teacher and student indicate the pressure on the fields of comparative and international education to recognise this world on the move. In the twenty-first century, such global movements and transformations, which in one way lock nationally shaped educational institutions together in a common global project, challenge us to think critically about our theoretical and methodological models, helping us break out of what Beck (2005) called 'methodological nationalism'.

Recent research on migration, mobilities and education has promoted alternative perspectives. There is increasing concern to deconstruct these two concepts by identifying the influence of psychological/social interpretations by migrant groups themselves of such issues – not just migrant adults but youth and children. A variety of methodological approaches allow us to widen the focus to be able to listen to the voices of migrant groups and individuals (Rao 2010). This has involved interpretative research, whether ethnographies or qualitative case studies (a few of which are presented in this special issue), and interdisciplinary research, which offer us the chance to explore the varied political, social and geographic/spatial experience and identities of migrants (Adams and Kirova 2007; Modood and Salt 2011). However, such methodological approaches are not unproblematic. Moving beyond a numerical measurement and linear analysis of migration, which seeks to identify its societal consequences, means that there is less emphasis on pattern and more on the specificity of experience that is relevant to different migrant communities, different generations, but also different sub-groups, such as migrant youth, students and children, migrant parents of children, teachers and academics. This plurality of sample, whilst reminding us of the kaleidoscope of migratory experiences, makes it difficult to develop strong generic conceptual frameworks.

The purpose of this special issue is to demonstrate a range of contemporary perspectives on how migration and mobility have impacted or can impact on education. Below, we locate the contributions within three major themes.

Poverty, migration, child mobility and social reproduction

Recent studies on migration, mobility and education consider the prevalence of poverty and wealth and different aspirations towards upward mobility within such unequal structures. Internal and external migration is often presented as a pathway towards upward social mobility and a means of escaping poverty, yet as Bryan Maddox (2010) argued, migration also carries risks for the poor, such as incomplete schooling and the loss of some initial advantage for the family, for example in terms of child labour or a means of livelihood. Thus, migration may be less about social mobility and more about the social reproduction of existing disadvantages within the country (Maddox 2010; McEvoy et al. 2012).

Maddox (2010) drew our attention to the limitations of our understanding of modernity and development, which can imply that education is only effective if it contributes to occupational mobility, increased income and possibly a break, even if temporary, from poverty. However, migration issues relating to education cannot simply be put into the pre-existing grid of human capital theory, credentialism or cost-benefit analysis. As he pointed out, not all the returns from migration are tangible and quantifiable – for example quantitative analysis of educational outcomes cannot tap the micro-changes associated with 'status, income and occupational identity' that the poor experience through education (Jeffery, Jeffery, and Jeffery 2008). Ideally, moving beyond formal measurements in terms of educational attainment or occupational position in the job market will mean that 'marginal returns' will be addressed and that these educational returns might even be identified where there are no prospects of employment (Maddox 2010, 215). For some migrants, this takes the form of what has been called a 'Faustian bargain':

> The opportunity for 'escape' through migration also entails risks for the poor. It may be viewed as last chance strategy … and may lead to the dissolution of the family as a viable social and economic unit. (Wood 2003, cited in Maddox 2010, 214)

Whilst it is important to recognise the issues and challenges faced by child migrants, both the loss suffered and the difficulties faced in a new environment and receiving country, it is equally necessary to acknowledge their agency in the process, at all phases of their trajectories, to overcome 'deficit models of educational interventions' (Adams and Kirova 2007, 326) and recognise their resilience (Boyden 2003, 2011). This migration/poverty/education nexus is addressed by the first two articles of this special issue, those by Jo Boyden and by Caroline Dyer, in two different scenarios in which the poor migrate – one in search of schooling, the other seeking schooling forms that validate rather than destroy their migratory cultures.

Jo Boyden's presidential address at the BAICE 2012 conference, published here, draws our attention to the fact that child mobility away from the family and their migration in search of schooling have considerable strategic relevance to the resourcing of poor families. Drawing on the insights gained from the massive data collected on some 3000 boys and girls born in the mid-1990s and in 2001–2002 by the Young Lives project from Ethiopia, India, Peru and Vietnam, Boyden highlights the impact of educational expansion and its associated aspirational shifts on this pattern of survival. Whilst in developed countries, schooling is associated with residentially fixed homes (except those rich who shop for boarding schools for their children abroad), in poor countries children in increasing numbers are leaving home alone to find secondary schools or just 'good schools'. In this scenario, 'education can be less a casualty than a driver of child migration'. High aspirations of a better life and social mobility lead to a physical search for school education that takes children far from their families. As she points out, 'the global link between school education and childhood mobility is becoming ever more apparent'.

Such 'independent child migration' is shown to raise a number of important questions for migration studies, not least the notions that such non-parent residence is a familial crisis, that childhood should be spatially restricted and that young people leaving home is a 'shame'. Boyden demonstrates through the data that child migrants show respect for their parents and elders since they aim to make a contribution to their family's income by improving their learning (a task that is fast becoming 'the children's chief familial responsibility'). They try to fulfil their family's collectively high aspirations of achieving a good education for them and of gaining a better life both psychologically and physically. Migrating in search of better schooling is a form of educational investment, whether in private or in government schools (Srivastava 2013), which, according to Boyden, is 'fundamental to mutual relations between generations'. Significantly, the movement between schools, on the one hand, and school transfers, on the other, is understood to be part of the global marketisation of education, leading to more interest in the patterns of school choice, new forms of residential accommodation and different forms of family/household–school connections.

The delivery of education through geographic catchment areas is challenged by this migratory practice. Boyden's analysis makes us consider whether the notion of entitlement to education promoted by EFA restrictively still builds on traditional models of formal schooling and educational opportunities. Similarly Caroline Dyer's paper 'Does Mobility Have to Mean Being Hard to Reach?' asks us to challenge EFA's assumptions about the sedentary nature of schooling. Drawing insights from her research in Western India on the Rabaris of Kuch, Dyer draws attention to the marginalisation associated with mobile pastoralists, a group that has been much neglected in studies on migration and education. The 2010 Education For All Global Monitoring Report (GMR) called for urgent action to address their educational deprivation. However, the terms 'nomad' and 'pastoralist' themselves, as Dyer argues, are also contested and debated notions, often interpreted within a deficit discourse.

To explore what Sen defines as 'ways of judging' injustice, Dyer builds on a livelihoods-orientated analysis (Scoones 2009) to examine the 'terms of inclusion' of institutional responses to pastoralists' educational deprivation around the world. She suggests that the models and institutional arrangements commonly offered for the education of mobile pastoralists contribute to their exclusion and marginalisation. A recognition of the 'livelihood sustainability' of pastoralism can help reframe the relationship of education to mobility and overcome the dichotomy between formalised education and 'situated livelihood learning'. Here, formal education would be '*complementary to*, rather than *in competition with*', the latter. This reconceptualisation of the terms in which 'social injustice is understood' has implications for the provision of education for mobile pastoralists and for wider understandings of issues of migration, education and mobility in contexts of chronic poverty.

Networks of migration within and across national educational systems

The second theme in this special issue refers to the very different experience of groups of migrants who find themselves for a range of different reasons, whether through forced migration or choice migration, studying in schools abroad. Here there is a multitude of issues to research, not least the educational and community experiences of migrant youth and students trying to make sense of their studies, their new lives and the structural conditions they face. These issues also include teachers who often feel unprepared to deal with the new diversity of children in schools. The curricular issues too are multiple: schools are carrying, as it were, the demographic challenges of globalisation whilst still embedded in their national histories and demands.

Not all countries that let in migrants and their families welcome them or promise integration. Indeed, Bauman (2004) called migrants the 'flotsam of globalisation' – part of the wasteland left over from wars, famines and industrial shifts globally. Migrants' experience of the school system in the receiving country is framed by the institutional cultures and pedagogic regimes of the school but also by immigration policy. The temporality of migration, as Rao (2010) points out, is critical to the experience of education. Time allows individuals and groups to stay but not to participate in civic membership and hence become fully integrated. Young people are particularly vulnerable here. They might come with parents on temporary visas, as trafficked or unaccompanied minors. What is often the case is that migrant students are 'non-citizens' in a twilight zone, without membership of society. Researching these migratory experiences is challenging, not least because poor and 'illegal' migrants are not easily identified. They may be rendered invisible formally by the state and also informally by a school system that does not want to stigmatise them (Pinson, Arnot, and Candappa 2010).

We know from research that the forms of marginalisation and 'othering' of migrant students inside schools and colleges are also underpinned by the unequal power hierarchies inscribed in nationalist and postcolonial imagery and memory (Bhabha 1994), which often shape policy and practice. These processes of exclusion are found not just in South/North migration – South-South migration also carries these forms of marginalisation and exclusion. Bartlett (2012) reminded us in an article in *Compare* of the exclusionary practices that make it impossible for young migrant Haitians to fit into Dominican society, where they experience physical and mental abuse and denial of the right papers to claim birth and citizenship, thus forcing some to drop out of school. South-South migration still has colonial history embedded in its notions of skin colour, which constructs 'black' as dangerous and 'bad' and views immigrant youth as deviant and a source of trouble. The implications for EFA and MDGs of these postcolonial processes of exclusion within schooling are fruitful topics for future research. Addressing the ethics of schooling, its structures, processes and teacher attitudes is critical to the well-being of young migrants within Southern states.

It is also important that research on the school experiences of migrant students recognises the importance of religion and language. Addressing religious diversity presents significant challenges for schools, but also for particular groups such as Muslim youth. These youth might not be 'migrants' in terms of temporality (they would be classified as second/third generation nationals rather than newly arrived); however, increased Islamophobia in schools in receiving countries, combined with an emphasis on security and the 'War on Terror', have created different conditions for the processes of identity formation, identification and belonging of such youth – they are being treated 'as if newly arrived'. These new conditions mean that religion has become the new identity marker, in some cases over other forms of national identification (Basit 2009; Shain 2011). In a context in which multiculturalism is being questioned across Europe (Vertovec and Wessendorf 2009), contemporary forms of religious discrimination and tensions in school carry broader social implications for migrant receiving societies.

The language issues associated with increased demographic movement are also ever more important for state schools whether in the global North or South, not least because the new so-called 'superdiversity' in schools in urban areas (Blommaert 2011) has meant that language has moved beyond an educational challenge to become a social and political one. The 'moral panic' around non-English-speaking children in schools, echoed by tabloids in Britain, exemplifies the new challenges faced by migrant students. Recent research emphasises the need for support in learning the language of the receiving country, whilst encouraging oracy and literacy in children's home languages (Mallows 2012). Studies have emphasised forms of curriculum innovation, and there is also a push towards more bilingual learning to build on children's skills in their home language, and encourage literacy development in both languages. These new perspectives, however, face strong challenges and point to the paradox of international migration: whilst flows of people have taken on a global dimension, national curricula on the whole remain embedded within strong national cultures. The question of how monocultural and monolingual school systems can embrace the new diversity offered by global migration is yet unanswered (Welply 2010; Blommaert 2011).

Kulyk's article in this edition examines such tensions and contradictions of school-based language policies within Ukraine, examining the situation of two minority linguistic groups in Ukraine: the Hungarians of Transcarpathia and the Crimean Tatars of the Crimean peninsula. The findings were based on research conducted in localities with majority and minority Hungarian populations and with Crimean Tatar minorities. Building on semi-structured interviews with education officials and minority activists, along with questionnaire responses of students in their final year of secondary school (grade 11) and their parents, Kulyk describes the policy approach to the education of minority languages for these groups, contrasting it with the beliefs of students and parents within these minority groups.

Kulyk contrasts the preservation of instruction in Hungarian language with the limited instruction in Crimean Tatar – both being problematic for the social integration and the ethnocultural identities of each group. The extensive instruction in Hungarian for this minority group creates problems in terms of integration within mainstream Ukrainian-speaking higher education and the labour market. Conversely, the restricted instruction in the language of the Crimean Tatar leads to a limited proficiency for young Crimean Tatars in the minority language, rendering their cultural identity more vulnerable. In light of these findings, the author argues in favour of bilingual education, which integrates instruction in the majority language (Ukranian) and in minority languages.

Another dimension of migrant student experience in 'receiving schools' is that of social/ethnic difference. New concepts such as 'ethnic capital' have been suggested to understand the experience of migrants in receiving societies in a context of increased globalisation (Modood and Salt 2011). Rao (2010) implies that credentials, even language credentials, are less important than social networks. The ethnic capital of migrant students and their communities are not just nationally contained, but part of a diaspora in which there is two-directional or even circular transmission of ideas. We are becoming more aware of the locking together of receiving and sending countries in diasporic educational networks that are more than the sending back of remittances. The article by Van der Linden and her colleagues in this special issue exemplifies this aspect of international migration – it shows us how fledging alliances were created between the South Sudanese diaspora in the Netherlands and their home base in Sudan. The ambition to help develop the educational system of one's home country creates a virtuous (if difficult) knowledge circle.

Building on a theoretical framework that combines capacity development, human capabilities and transnationalism, the authors identify the opportunities and challenges of the micro-development educational projects in South Sudan, initiated by the South Sudanese diaspora. The authors conducted a review of relevant policy documents, participated as observers in seminars, meetings and celebrations of the South Sudanese diaspora in the Netherlands and interviewed the main initiators of three projects. The commitment of members of the South Sudanese diaspora to participate in the reconstruction of public infrastructure, especially schools, in South Sudan appears as a form of compensation to their home country, albeit with different goals – education for peace-building, education to provide a safe environment or education to develop self-sustenance. Diasporas, understood as 'the people living the social phenomenon of transnationalism', can play a central role in these forms of capacity development partnerships, both through their knowledge of the local context and through their commitment and loyalty to their home country.

Higher education and international student mobility: concerns and opportunities

In contrast to the study of migrant students in schools, research on global migration in higher education is fast becoming an established field of research (see, for example, Robinson-Pant 2005, 2009; Gu, Schweisfurth, and Day 2009). Bileçen's article in this special issue offer new insights into the relationship between education and social reproduction by exploring international postgraduate students' identifications with local nationals in Germany, whilst Kadiwal and Rind make a thoughtful contribution to the study of migrating offshore education in the Middle East by focusing on the tensions within transnational knowledge adaptations.

Studies within higher education tend again to reflect *either* macro analyses emphasising economic and organisational factors (see, for example, Martens, Rusconi, and Leuze 2007) *or* research regarding students' (and teachers') experiences, identification processes and future intentions in the wider social context (e.g. Gu, Schweisfurth, and Day 2009; Robinson-Pant 2005, 2009). Identity here is not seen as a static notion, but is viewed as a continuous social process that involves negotiations between different, at times conflicting, and changing experiences and values. In this context, Anna Robinson-Pant's review (included in this special issue) of Brooks and Waters' (2011) book on student mobilities, migration and the internationalisation of higher education raises important points. Brooks and Waters' emphasis on identity construction, new networks and different kinds of cultural capital held by international students, especially from the South, encourage us to move away from focusing on the one-way transfer of students (i.e., a linear approach) to think about the transnational interconnections between globalisation, migration and knowledge construction.

Both Bileçen's and Kadiwal and Rind's paper in this special issue contribute to the debate about international students' identification processes. Bileçen's article is based on semi-structured interviews with international doctoral students in two universities in Germany and highlights the students' engagement with different 'Others'. The interesting aspect is that these 'Others' are not only defined as German nationals (external difference) but also as the students' co-nationals who share the same nationality, ethnicity, language and 'in some instances even the same class' and who also live in Germany (internal differences). This internal differentiation from co-nationals was reflected by the majority of respondents from China, the Philippines, Mexico, Russia and Turkey. The author thus highlights the diverse status of immigrant groups and the ways in which well-educated migrant groups counter the 'cultural stereotypes perpetuated by mainstream society', whilst at the same time stereotyping members of the same community living in Germany, thus adding to the latter's social inequality and exclusion. Migrant students in higher education may therefore contribute to internal social class differentiation in the receiving society.

The article 'Selective Cosmopolitans: Tutors and Students' Experience of Offshore Higher Education in Dubai', by Kadiwal and Rind, included here, explores the experience of international postgraduate students and their teachers in a different setting – that of the 'UK University' in Dubai. Many of their interviewees migrated to Dubai from countries such as Egypt, Lebanon and Palestine to participate in this offshore education. This model of education is financially lucrative for universities but it also offers opportunities for such students to stay in their country or region rather than travelling abroad to the 'host' university. However, here there are cultural-political tensions such as that between such offshore education and the local culture (see also Rizvi 2010; Miller-Idriss and Hanauer 2011). These authors focus on the adaptation of the UK Post-Graduate Certificate in Education for Dubai, conducting in-depth, semi-structured interviews with tutors and students. They uncover complex negotiation processes and difficult linguistic and cultural political dimensions. The authors suggest that the tutors from the UK and the international students reflect a selective cosmopolitanism whereby 'central tensions surrounding language and culture' are negotiated strategically and ambivalently (Skrbis and Woodward 2007).

Conclusion

The authors in this special issue in different ways strongly emphasise the fluidity, diversity and complexity of the terms migration and mobility. Using social constructionist approaches, each in turn emphasises processes relating to agency, negotiation, identification and differentiation, whether these are to meet family obligations, sustain livelihoods, negotiate language, aspire to social mobility or create global partnerships. Thus, whilst Boyden explores the negotiation of schooling as a benefit for the family, Dyer considers the negative discourses that have to be negotiated by those who do not fit the sedentary culture of schooling. Kulyk highlights the interconnectedness of negotiating language diversity within unequal structures, whilst Van der Linden taps into the interconnectedness of diasporas with their home country's education system, negotiating change. Kadiwal and Rind develop Skrbis and Woodward's (2007) notion of the ambivalent and strategic cosmopolitan in the Dubai setting of offshore education and Bileçen uses internal and external differentiation to decipher the identification processes of international students in Germany.

Analysing the formation of education networks and processes, whether across the rural-urban divide, within migratory communities and diasporas or across the global North and South, is critical to the politics and governance of education within a globalised world. Network examples (whether the establishment of new bonds, the use of existing networks or differentiation from possible common identities) in this special issue are only the tip of the iceberg. Migration is not linear, it is part of the global civil society and resistances therefore take global shape. Underlying the discussions in these papers is the notion of transnationalism, which a number of authors have referred to. This concept 'broadly refers to multiple ties and interactions linking people or institutions across the borders of nation-states' (Vertovec 1999, 447). Transnationalism is seen as an important aspect of integration (see Vertovec 2010), although not the same – the nation-state remains an important analytical category (amongst others) in so far as the structures and systems (e.g. economic, political, legal, etc.) of the nation state, and of the countries-of-origin, third countries and receiving countries, contextualise the agency of people who are affected by these structures and systems and maintain or change them via their actions (see Schneider 2012). This special issue encourages us to explore the interconnectedness of such national structures, patterns of negotiation, voice and agency, and also to redefine our analysis of the effects and benefits of migration as a social process.

References

Adams, L., and A. Kirova, eds. 2007. *Global Migration and Education*. Mahwah, NJ: Laurence Erlbaum Associates.

Bartlett, L. 2012. "South-South Migration and Education: The Case of People of Haitian Descent Born in the Dominican Republic." *Compare* 42 (3): 393–414.

Basit, T. 2009. "White British; Dual Heritage; British Muslim: Young Britons' Conceptualisation of Identity and Citizenship." *British Educational Research Journal* 35 (5): 723–743. doi:10.1080/01411920802688747.

Bauman, Z. 2004. *Wasted Lives: Modernity and Its Outcast*. Cambridge: Polity Press.

Beck, U. 2005. *Power in the Global Age: A New Global Political Economy*. Translated by K. Cross. Malden, MA: Cambridge Polity.

Bhabha, H. 1994. *The Location of Culture*. London: Routledge.

Blommaert, J. 2011. *Sociolinguistics of Globalization*. Cambridge: Cambridge University Press.

Boyden, J. 2003. "Children under Fire: Challenging Assumptions about Children's Resilience." *Children, Youth and Environments* 13 (1). http://www.colorado.edu/journals/cye/13_1/Vol13_1Articles/CYE_CurrentIssue_Article_ChildrenUnderFire_Boyden.htm

Boyden, J. 2011. "Why Resilience Research Needs to Take Account of Political Economy and Culture." *International Society for the Study of Behavioural Development Bulletin* 59 (1): 27–31.

Brooks, R., and J. Waters. 2011. *Student Mobilities, Migration and the Internationalization of Higher Education*. Basingstoke: Palgrave Macmillan. doi:10.1057/9780230305588.

Cao, X. 1996. "Debating 'Brain Drain' in the Context of Globalisation." *Compare* 26 (3): 269–285.

Demirdjian, L., ed. 2012. *Education, Refugees and Asylum Seekers*. London: Continuum.

Gu, Q., M. Schweisfurth, and C. Day. 2009. "Learning and Growing in a 'Foreign' Context: Intercultural Experiences of International Students." *Compare* 40 (1): 1–17.

Jeffrey, C., P. Jeffery, and R. Jeffery. 2008. *Degrees without Freedom? Education, Masculinities and Unemployment in North India*. Stanford, CA: University of Stanford Press.

Maddox, B. 2010. "Marginal Returns: Re-Thinking Mobility and Educational Benefit in Contexts of Chronic Poverty." *Compare: A Journal of Comparative and International Education* 40 (2): 213–222. doi:10.1080/03057920903546070.

Mallows, D., ed. 2012. *Innovations in English Language Teaching for Migrants and Refugees*. London: British Council.

Martens, K., A. Rusconi, and K. Leuze. 2007. *New Arenas of Education Governance: The Impact of International Organizations and Markets on Educational Policy Making*. Basingstoke: Palgrave Macmillan.

McEvoy, J., P. Petrzelka, C. Radel, and B. Schmook. 2012. "Gendered Mobility and Morality in a South-Eastern Mexican Community: Impacts of Male Labour Migration on the Women Left Behind." *Mobilities* 7(3): 369–388. doi:10.1080/17450101.2012.655977.

Miller-Idriss, C., and E. Hanauer. 2011. "Transnational Higher Education: Offshore Campuses in the Middle-East." *Comparative Education* 47 (2): 181–207. doi:10.1080/03050068.2011.553935.

Modood, T., and J. Salt. 2011. *Global Migration, Ethnicity and Britishness*. Basingstoke: Palgrave Macmillan. doi:10.1057/9780230307155.

Pinson, H., M. Arnot, and M. Candappa. 2010. *Education, Asylum and the 'Non-Citizen' Child*. London: Palgrave Macmillan. doi:10.1057/9780230276505.

Rao, N. 2010. "Migration, Education and Socio-Economic Mobility." *Compare: A Journal of Comparative and International Education* 40 (2): 137–145. doi:10.1080/03057920903545973.

Rizvi, F. 2010. "International Students and Doctoral Studies in Transnational Spaces." In *The Routledge Doctoral Supervisor's Companion: Supporting Effective Research in Education and the Social Sciences*, edited by M. Walker and P. Thomson, 158–170. Abingdon: Routledge.

Robinson-Pant, A. 2005. *Cross-Cultural Perspectives on Educational Research.* Buckingham: Open University Press.

Robinson-Pant, A. 2009. "Changing Academies: Exploring International Phd Students' Perspectives on 'Host' and 'Home' Universities." *Higher Education Research and Development* 28 (4): 417–429.

Rutter, J. 1999. *Refugee Children in the UK.* Milton Keyns: Open University Press.

Schneider, C. 2012. "A Theoretical Discussion of Formulating a Middle-Range Theory of Transnationalism and Education." Paper presented at the British Association for International and Comparative Education Conference 2012, Churchill College, Cambridge, September 8–10.

Scoones, I. 2009. "Livelihoods Perspectives and Rural Development." *Journal of Peasant Studies* 36 (1): 171–196. doi:10.1080/03066150902820503.

Shain, F. 2011. *The New Folk Devils: Muslim Boys and Education in England.* Stoke-on-Trent: Trentham Books.

Skrbis, Z., and I. Woodward. 2007. "The Ambivalence of Ordinary Cosmopolitanism: Investigating the Limits of Cosmopolitan Openness." *The Sociological Review* 55 (4): 731–747.

Srivastava, P. 2013. *Low-Fee Private Schooling; Aggravating Equity or Mitigating Disadvantage?* Oxford: Symposium Books.

Vertovec, S. 1999. "Conceiving and Researching Transnationalism." *Ethnic and Racial Studies* 22 (2): 447–462. doi:10.1080/014198799329558.

Vertovec, S. 2010. "Towards Post-Multiculturalism? Changing Communities, Conditions and Contexts of Diversity." *International Social Science Journal* 61 (199): 83–95. doi:10.1111/issj.2010.61.

Vertovec, S., and S. Wessendorf, eds. 2009. *The Multiculturalism Backlash: European Discourses, Policies, and Practices.* London: Routledge.

Welply, O. 2010. "Language Difference and Identity in Multicultural Classrooms: The Views of 'Immigrant-Background' Children in French and English Primary Schools." *Compare* 40 (3): 345–358. doi:http://dx.doi.org/10.1080/03057920903395502.

World Bank. 2011. *Migration and Remittances Factbook 2011.* Washington, DC: World Bank.

Madeleine Arnot
University of Cambridge, Cambridge, UK

Claudia Schneider
Anglia Ruskin University, Cambridge, UK

Oakleigh Welply
University of Cambridge, Cambridge, UK

'We're not going to suffer like this in the mud': educational aspirations, social mobility and independent child migration among populations living in poverty

Jo Boyden

Department of International Development, University of Oxford, Oxford, UK

This article examines the association between formal education, social mobility and independent child migration in Ethiopia, India (Andhra Pradesh), Peru and Vietnam and draws on data from Young Lives, a longitudinal study of childhood poverty and schooling. It argues that among resource-poor populations, child migration sustains kin relations across generations and households and also facilitates children's progression through the life-course, thus it is fundamental to social reproduction. It reasons that formal education has greatly amplified this trend. Schooling has acquired symbolic value as the prime means of escaping household poverty and realising ambitions for social mobility. As such, elevated educational aspirations combine with systems shortcomings to stimulate school selection, school transfer and school-related child migration. The article concludes by examining the implications for children, for social reproduction and for policy.

Introduction

The link globally between school education and childhood mobility is becoming ever more apparent. Yet in orthodox scholarly accounts this association unsettles cherished ideals with regard to the child, the family and the school and the role of family and formal education in the care and socialisation of the young. Parental proximity and the residentially fixed home having become naturalised as essential to child wellbeing, child movement away from the home is represented through discourses of family rupture and dysfunction (critiqued in Ni Laoire et al. 2010; Serra 2009; Whitehead, Hashim, and Iversen 2007). Likewise, the relationship between child mobility and formal education, when it is considered, is most often framed in the negative, as precipitating educational failure or school abandonment (for example, McKenzie and Rapoport 2006; Smita 2008). In effect, only in the boarding school tradition is separation from parents for didactic purposes accepted as legitimate practice.

Drawing on qualitative data from Young Lives,[1] a mixed-methods cohort study of childhood poverty and schooling in Ethiopia, India (in the state of Andhra Pradesh), Peru and Vietnam, this article explores the relationship between schooling and child mobility from a rather different perspective. It maintains that in contexts of poverty, child mobility is less an anathema and more a fundamental feature of social reproduction, the recent expansion of formal education magnifying this circumstance. The article makes an analytical link between poverty, educational aspirations, ambitions for social mobility and children's physical mobility. In doing so, it uses the terms 'mobility' and 'migration' interchangeably to refer both to children departing solo from the natal home and to non-parental residence.[2] It finds that familial social mobility is increasingly thought to depend on children's education, raised educational aspirations producing a demand for schooling that is relevant, of good quality and has social worth. In this way, school systems inadequacies, perceived and actual, have led to the commoditisation of education, manifested in dual enrolment, extra tuition, school selection, school transfers and school-related child migration. The article concludes that education can therefore be less a casualty than a driver of child migration.

Section 1 outlines the case for conceptualising child mobility as a central feature of social reproduction and highlights the part played by formal education. Section 2 briefly describes the Young Lives research design. Section 3 examines educational aspirations and delivery in the study countries. Section 4 outlines the evidence on school selection, school transfers and school-related child migration. The final section highlights the implications of these processes for children's social integration and learning, for social reproduction and for educational planning more broadly.

1. Independent child migration: a theoretical challenge?

Migration has become a major area of social science enquiry in recent decades, recognised as associated with widespread societal transformation and economic development (Maddox 2010). Yet migration research has taken little account of children's mobility (Ni Laoire et al. 2010; Whitehead, Hashim, and Iversen 2007). The assumption has been that, as household dependents, children remain with their biological parents under all normal circumstances, either accompanying them during relocation or continuing in the natal home when a parent stays behind. Underlying this assumption is the idea that children's physical immaturity is invariably coupled with developmental vulnerability, their healthy growth and social adjustment contingent upon sustained emotional attachments and physical proximity with parents (Schaffer 1999). In this way, child relocation from the natal home is repeatedly conflated in the literature with familial crisis, child exploitation, trafficking and developmental risk (for example Boonpala and Kane 2001; for a critique, Boyden and Howard 2013).

Recent empirical work has presented a very different picture, making clear that, in practice, childhood is envisioned, structured and experienced in divergent ways across the globe. Specifically, research within geography, anthropology and related disciplines has highlighted the spatiality of childhood experience and provided plentiful evidence that both child mobility and non-parental residence are customary in many parts of the world (see, for example, Ansell and van Blerk 2004; Hashim 2007; Hashim and Thorsen 2011; Heissler 2013; Huijsmans 2008; Leinaweaver 2008; Punch 2007; Whitehead, Hashim, and Iversen 2007). Child mobility is closely associated with rural modes of social organisation and commonly prevails in areas that cannot guarantee household subsistence or meet young people's social ambitions (Rao 2010b). Indeed, in parts of West Africa it is so widespread that there can be shame in young people remaining at home (Akua Anyidoho and Ainsworth 2009). This evidence brings into question the 'powerful ideologies that place idealised childhoods in fixed and bounded spaces' (Ni Laoire et al. 2010, 157), as well as the depiction of children as mere family dependents, or 'luggage' (Orellana et al. 2001), during migration. It also provides important insights for theorising the association between household poverty, child migration and school education.

To better appreciate this link, it is necessary to understand the wider logic underlying child relocation and non-parental residence among populations experiencing poverty. Briefly, inasmuch as it safeguards the care, development and economic contribution of the young, children's migration plays a central role in both the individual life-course and the domestic cycle and is therefore less an expression of familial dysfunction than a fundamental attribute of social reproduction. Starting with its part in the life-course, independent migration has long been one of the chief means by which boys and girls fulfil their multiple responsibilities towards their family. The young are seldom simply household dependents in contexts of poverty and more often active participants in domestic economic and care regimes (Robson et al. 2006; Spittler and Bourdillon 2012). Particularly significant for the present discussion, contributing to the household not only supports young people's learning and development (Bourdillon et al. 2010) but also enables them to demonstrate respect for parents and elders (Heissler and Porter forthcoming). Children's familial contributions have both instrumental and symbolic value, helping fulfil immediate domestic requirements and also serving collective ambitions for the future, through the prospect of a financial or social return to their future employment or marriage.

Less disruptive to domestic economies and organisation than whole families moving away, independent child migration is especially common in rural areas with low or declining agricultural productivity and limited employment opportunities. Children's movement is commonly articulated through close ties of kinship, friendship and shared community of origin (Giani 2006; Heissler 2013). Since it entails leaving the natal home alone and/or assuming proto-adult roles at the place of destination, child relocation can occasion significant life-course changes. For example, it may facilitate entry into paid work (Iversen 2002), the learning of new trades and skills (Ansell and van Blerk 2004; Dobson 2009; Dougnon 2012; Hashim 2007) or autonomous living (Rao 2010a). This evidence has led to the theorisation of independent child migration as a life transition event (Punch 2007). In terms of the part played by child mobility in the domestic cycle, young people relocating is very often an outcome of dispersed familial networks in which separate households are interdependent economically and socially and to varying degrees, pool labour, income, goods and social care (for example Alber 2003; Ansell and van Blerk 2004; van Blerk 2005; Boyden and Howard 2013; Hashim 2007). So, the young may move to a household that offers nurturance, sponsorship or learning opportunities that are not available in the natal home or, alternatively, to augment the labour of a host household that has shortages. In this way, child relocation sustains productive and reproductive labour and reinforces familial ties across both generations and households.

The main thesis of this article is that the recent expansion of school systems and associated escalation in educational aspirations have intensified child mobility among populations living in poverty. Within the context of the global rise of the 'knowledge economy', formal education has become the defining feature of modern childhood (Crivello 2009, 395–396), commonly perceived of as the prime path out of poverty, to expanded opportunity and to broader societal transformation (Froerer 2011; Rao 2010a). In providing a major focus for collective social aspirations, schooling increasingly competes with, and is gradually superseding, work as children's prime familial responsibility. At the same time, with uneven education access, quality and relevance and with individual schools being awarded different social worth, schooling has become progressively more commoditised, the subject of preferences and choice that give impetus to school transfers and, ultimately, independent child migration.

The education-related motives for boys and girls migrating are very varied. They include the search for better quality schooling (Bano 2007; Giani 2006), the possibility, especially in rural areas, of entering secondary school (Ansell 2004; Porter et al. 2011) or of working to cover school expenses (Punch 2007). Rural schooling may also prompt relocation when it fails to serve employment aspirations or is perceived as needlessly prolonging dependence (Ofosu-Kusi and Mizen 2012). Often children relocate to families that are better able to sponsor their schooling (Zimmerman 2003) or willing to support their education in exchange for their labour (Hashim 2007). Migration for education may give rise to social parenthood through fosterage (Alber 2003) and in some contexts fostered children are more likely than others to attend school (Zimmerman 2003, 558). Thus, the literature points to school-related incentives for child migration as ranging from economic or mentoring opportunities to constraints in the natal home and systems shortcomings in the immediate locality. This article focuses on the part played by educational aspirations and systems weaknesses in Ethiopia, Andhra Pradesh and Peru (and to a lesser extent Vietnam). Before providing the evidence and analysis, it briefly outlines the Young Lives research design.

2. Young Lives[3]

In each of the study countries, Young Lives is following 2000 boys and girls born in 2001–2002 and up to 1000 born in 1994–1995 over 15 years. The children were selected randomly from 20 rural and urban sites per country that were chosen from amongst the poorest regions nationally. So far, three survey rounds have been administered to the full sample of children, their caregivers and community representatives, in 2002, 2006 and 2009 and three rounds of qualitative data have been gathered from a sub-sample of children from both age cohorts, in 2007, 2008 and 2011. The qualitative methods comprise semi-structured interviews, focus groups, drawing (including community mapping and life-course draw-and-tell), writing (a daily activity diary) and photo elicitation. In the survey, questions on schooling history, parental involvement in children's education and parental aspirations for children's education are complemented by information on children's time use and academic achievement and, in rounds two and three, desired levels of education. The qualitative research covers children's attitudes towards and experiences of poverty, their sense of well-being and ill-being and hopes for the future, as well as their roles and social and institutional transitions. School-based research was introduced in 2010, enabling examination of the educational experiences of Young Lives children at key stages in their educational careers.

Child migration was not central to the initial research design and at the time of recruitment into the study the child respondents were all living with their families. Moreover, across the sample, the majority of boys and girls who attend school have remained within the catchment area. However, a number of children, some of whom are in the qualitative sub-sample, have relocated for their studies and many have siblings who are studying elsewhere. Also, many express a desire to migrate, either to be able to continue their education or to access a better school, and in Andhra Pradesh many are either enrolled in more than one school or have transferred between schools several times, while some are boarding. It is not possible to determine the incidence or trends in school transfers or school-related mobility from the survey data because the broad reach of topics covered limits the opportunity for detailed questioning on specific subjects and also because the wide variation in the duration, nature and conceptualisation of migratory processes leads to significant underreporting. Therefore, this article draws on qualitative data obtained mainly from the older cohort and their caregivers.

3. The drivers of mobility

Educational aspirations and delivery

The economies of the four study countries grew significantly between 2002 and 2009. In all cases, economic growth has been associated with national expansion of formal education and with high levels of school enrolment among children in the Young Lives sample. Thus, in 2002, at 97% or above, primary school enrolment was near-universal across Andhra Pradesh, Peru and Vietnam (Murray 2012). Systems expansion has been complemented by a range of measures to boost school participation, including advocacy, compulsion and incentives. In line with these promotional efforts and with schooling progressively serving wider social ambitions, Young Lives children and caregivers express high levels of commitment to formal education. Thus, for example, even though it is a pro-poor sample, more than half of the parents of eight-year-olds in Ethiopia, Peru and Vietnam wanted their child to complete university (Pells 2011). Moreover, the survey data reveal considerable coherence between caregivers' ambitions for their children's education and children's own educational ambitions in all four study countries. Dercon and Singh (2013) found a striking association between caregivers' educational aspirations for children when they were aged 8 and children's aspirations for themselves at age 15. They also observed that children with higher aspirations at age 15 were more likely to be enrolled at that age.

One of the most notable features of raised aspirations is the perception that school education is both the sole means of escaping poverty and the prime vector for social mobility. For girls in Andhra Pradesh, this is often about obtaining sufficient education to enhance their prospects of marrying an educated man. This reasoning was clearly articulated by Harika, who is from the cotton growing area of Poompuhar and recently moved to a government hostel so that she could attend college:

> You get better jobs if you study and you have a better life and can marry an educated husband. If your husband is in agriculture, you have to go to the fields and work. If he is educated, you can be happy. We see our parents working and we feel that we do not want to be like them. They work in the fields and work hard every day.

In Andhra Pradesh there is considerable diversity in types of school and a recent escalation in low-fee private options has elevated educational aspirations, greatly influencing school choice. Measuring the educational level and job parents would like their children to obtain, Galab et al. (forthcoming) find that the children whose parents aspire for them to remain longer in education are more likely to attend private school. They also report that the magnitude of the increase in probability of private school enrolment is much higher when parents plan for their children to go to university and/or work in a high-status or high-income occupation.

Elevated educational aspirations are evident among children and caregivers throughout the qualitative sub-sample, across all four countries. The most consistent narrative along these lines comes from rural Peru. Crivello (2010) argues that, though most rely on their children's work, there is widespread consensus among rural caregivers in Peru that school education offers an escape from the drudgery of herding and farming, a path to wealth and material security and a means of releasing future generations from the hardship and suffering that they have endured. Recognised as the channel through which to become a 'professional', or somebody of social significance, education is also understood to enable children to better defend themselves and cope with life's challenges. One caregiver used the metaphor of footwear to symbolise the potential for inter-generational social transformation that he associates with education: 'I ... walk in the fields with sandals. At least he will go with shoes if he gets a good head with education' (Crivello 2010, 404).

A second Peruvian caregiver indicated that, '[children] have to study. I don't want [him] to be like me ...', while a third remarked: '*senora*, my daughter is not meant to work in the field'. Children in Peru share these perceptions. One girl articulated displeasure at having to work on her family's farm, which she finds tiring, and wants to be a nurse. She told her mother, 'We're not going to suffer like this in the mud ... it's better that I go and study.' Another remarked that she finds working on her parents' farm disagreeable because her clothes get dirty and she feels 'shattered' at the end of the day. Though she acknowledges that her parents are reliant on her help, she stated, 'I am not going to be a peasant' and was adamant that, given her ambition to study nursing in Lima, the skills she has acquired through farm work will not serve her in the future.

Many parents make significant sacrifices to furnish their children with an education, as illustrated by two cases from Andhra Pradesh. At age 16, Harika gave up paid work in the cotton fields to return to school. The school entrance fee was 3600 rupees and the family spends a further 500–600 rupees monthly on her education, these being significant outgoings given their poverty. Likewise, despite facing many hardships, all of the children in Preethi's family, including Preethi herself, are studying and none are working. Preethi is from one of the many tribal groups in India that remain highly marginalised economically and socially, despite numerous measures of positive discrimination by government. Her mother described the family as being 'in a lot of trouble' financially. Her father is an alcoholic and when last interviewed the family had experienced several major setbacks – they would normally benefit from the National Rural Employment Guarantee Scheme, but this was suspended due to the heavy rains, and the grandfather's pension payments had also been stopped. Their eldest daughter was ill with malaria and typhoid and paying for her treatment, together with expenses incurred by building their house and conducting several ceremonies, had pushed the family into debt. So, to keep the children in school, the mother had to halt the construction work and sell some land and goats.

Whatever the ambitions, actual school attendance hinges on perceptions of the costs and benefits, which may vary according to a wide range of factors, including the attributes of the local labour market and opportunities for marriage. Choices may differ according to a child's gender or birth order, this revealing an invidious dimension to demand for formal education wherein families do not always place a high value on schooling for all (see also Alber 2012). In Andhra Pradesh, the returns to girls' education are felt to be much lower than for boys because girls are less likely to obtain well-paid jobs and more likely to cease to contribute to the natal home when they marry, which can be at quite a young age. As a consequence, Andhra Pradesh is the one context in the study where a systematic gender bias in educational investments is observed, with girls increasingly disadvantaged as compared with boys as they grow older (Dercon and Singh 2013). Harika's mother was explicit about the disincentives involved:

> We wanted to stop her from further studies. … Will she give us money once she starts working? Who will she give it to? We won't make anything from her. She is better off working here …..

She made reference to the financial problems the family faced, which included the interest they were paying on loans, their inability to plant cotton because of heavy rains and the hospitalisation of a son. She went on to underline the social pressures against educating girls: '… people are scolding us. They say: "What is the need to educate girls? They will get spoilt."' Accordingly, Harika struggled to convince her parents to let her stay on at school and delay marriage.

Harika's case is quite unusual for the children in the sub-sample for in interviews with adults and children across all four countries the prevailing perception is that educational investments and associated returns are fundamental to mutual relations between generations. Understood as the path to poverty relief and social mobility for the whole family, school success is fast becoming children's chief familial responsibility. A boy from Peru outlined this logic in terms of rewarding the sacrifices made by parents and elders to get their children educated:

> The young man who does well is studious, diligent and responsible, and has outstanding grades. He dreams of completing his higher education to have a career and to 'return the favour' of his parents, helping them when they are older.

That schooling is now key to sustaining kinship reciprocity with the promise of lifting families out of poverty can be seen in the case of Fanus, from the very different setting of Ethiopia. Fanus explained, 'I have to learn, be in a better position and improve my family's life.' She hopes to achieve this aim by becoming a doctor and has moved to a nearby town, to live in rented accommodation with her sister, so that she can remain at school. Her mother, who has been a single parent since the father abandoned the family some years back, is determined to ensure that her daughters complete their schooling and remarked that when she does so, Fanus must, 'pay her debt as I have done to her'. Thus, doing well at school is in large part about honouring children's responsibilities towards their parents.

The educational landscape

Strategies for realising educational aspirations are strongly contingent on the nature of the educational landscape, which varies hugely both between and within countries and according to a range of other factors, including national policies on migration. Key to the current discussion is that with educational expectations running so high, uneven coverage, quality and relevance of formal education, together with variations in perceived social worth of specific institutions, can stimulate school selection, school transfers and school-related child mobility.

There are official constraints on migration in Ethiopia and most pupils attend local public schools, many in half-day shifts that allow them to work. However, children tend to enrol late, attend intermittently, progress slowly and leave early having acquired few skills (Frost and Rolleston 2011). Thus, for example, while enrolment among Young Lives children at age 8 increased from 66% in 2002 to 77% in 2009 in Ethiopia, the literacy rate increased by only 2 percentage points during the same period (Woldehanna et al. 2011). Moreover, though 89.6% of the older cohort of children was still enrolled at age 15 to 16 years, only 18% had completed primary education at that point (Woldehanna et al. 2011). Due to severe limitations on coverage and quality, a growing proportion of rural children relocate for secondary schooling, even if only informally, or by moving short distances, or seasonally.

In Vietnam there is an explicit policy of universal provision that is relatively uniform in quality nationally. Also, migration for education is curbed by restrictions on access to schools in destination communities. Most pupils attend government schools and half-day shifts are common, with private tuition more customary than mobility as a means of supplementing local provision. Ethnic minority children living in the remote and mountainous northern region of Vietnam are the one population group that is encouraged to migrate to attend government hostel schools. Moreover, it is possible that sizeable disparities in school experience between ethnic majority and ethnic minority children in the Young Lives sample (Le Thuc et al. 2011) could constitute an added incentive for school-related migration among minority children. Thus, in both age groups, ethnic-minority children fare far less well in the acquisition of mathematics and reading skills than ethnic-majority Kinh children (Glewwe, Chen, and Katare 2012). Vu (forthcoming, 20) points to the use of an unfamiliar language, poor teaching methods, unwelcoming school environments and family poverty as key determinants of poor performance among Cham H'roi children.

Peru has a well-established public education system and most children go to government schools, with some, in urban areas especially, attending private schools. Though public education coverage is practically universal at the primary level, rural children may be forced to migrate to towns for secondary education. This has become a part of a much wider trend of abandonment of the countryside and rural ways of life as people move to urban areas in search of enhanced opportunities for themselves and their children. At the same time, serious disparities in education quality, which consistently advantage better-off children in the Young Lives sample (Cueto, Leon, and Muñoz forthcoming, 15), are likely to be a factor in school selection and school-related migration in a proportion of cases.

Though the policy in India has long been that every village should have a school within a kilometre's distance, boarding school education for social elites is an important feature of the country's colonial heritage. There exist a number of elite boarding schools (some of which are public) that have long been seen as a gold standard worth travelling for. Further, the Government implicitly encourages school movement and independent child migration in two specific ways. First, the sheer multiplicity of schools, many of which lie outside the catchment area and/or the public sector, combines with wide variation in school experiences to boost both school selection and mobility between schools. In Andhra Pradesh, attendance and progression to secondary and tertiary education levels are major challenges among disadvantaged groups and regions and completion of primary education is no guarantee of mastery of basic literacy and numeracy (Rolleston and James forthcoming). Consequently, parents strive to identify schools across private and government sectors that they can afford and believe will deliver on their aspirations (James and Woodhead forthcoming). Seemingly, the highest incidence of school selection and movement occurs in urban areas, where there is a greater supply of more diverse schools in the vicinity and households have larger income to cover fees (James and Woodhead forthcoming). Second, tribal and other socially marginalised groups living in remote rural areas can often only access education by moving into government hostel schools outside their communities. Consequently, child relocation for schooling appears to be more common in rural areas where it aligns with government policy on the national integration of minority groups.

Thus far it has been argued that with educational aspirations running so high, schooling has become an important feature of childhood. Yet government policies and school realities can result in very variable educational landscapes, in some cases presenting significant incentives for school selection, school transfers and school-related child migration. Andhra Pradesh has seen a rapid growth in low-fee private schools teaching through the medium of the English language. Bolstered by the belief that a command of English will enhance employment prospects and that private schools are superior to government facilities, this escalation has led to an upsurge in movement between schools and accelerated the commodification of education.

Already at pre-school level the majority of younger cohort children in urban areas of Andhra Pradesh, including 34% of those in the poorest quintile, were in private facilities (Streuli, Vennam, and Woodhead 2011; Woodhead and Streuli 2013). By the time they had reached around seven to eight years of age, 44% of these children were found to be attending private school, which was a rise from 24% of the older cohort who were in private facilities at the same age seven years earlier. James and Woodhead (forthcoming) report a threefold increase in the incidence of younger cohort children being moved between schools by the age of eight, compared with the older cohort at the same age. These figures exclude all school moves linked to 'regular' school transitions and household relocation, as well as the many school moves during the pre-school years. Choices are being made between government and private schools, between different private schools and, in some cases, between different types of government school (1). James and Woodhead conclude that in this context, selecting a school 'is not about a singular decision made at the transition points into pre-school or primary school. Instead, an increasing number of parents make multiple, successive choices even during their children's earliest schooling' (7–8).

The provision of boarding facilities in government hostels and residential schools for Scheduled Tribe children and other groups living in remote areas of Andhra Pradesh has been an inducement for school-related child migration. Instruction, food, utensils, accommodation and healthcare are all free and quite a few of the children in the sample have taken advantage of this policy, some even at the primary level. Their motives vary, as can be seen from the three examples cited below.

Balakrishna, a Scheduled Tribe boy in the younger cohort, is currently in fourth grade and has switched school three times, most recently moving from a local government facility to an Ashram school some distance away. His parents felt he needed closer supervision: 'The problem is, we do not stay at home during the day and they keep roaming without studying when we are not there. That is why we put them there, so that they will study well.' They plan to send him to a government school in the city of Hydera-bad when he reaches seventh grade. Balakrishna was content to leave the village school since the food and teaching were poor and enjoys living in the hostel, where he sleeps on the floor with 30 other boys.

Likewise, Preethi is studying in a government school and lives in a hos-tel with two other girls from her village. She and her two brothers having moved away to continue their education, her elder sister is the only one liv-ing at home and helping their parents farm. While her mother regrets that her children have moved away, Preethi is more sanguine: 'They accuse us at home for remaining idle and for not doing any work. … It is a great relief to be in school….' On the other hand, she found it hard to adjust to hostel life and is quite ambivalent about her circumstances: '… it is a tor-ture at school. … There the teachers keep chiding and taunting us. They accuse us for not studying. … Then we feel like coming back home as the nagging is unbearable for us.'

Balasubramanyam, who is in the younger cohort, was sent to an Ashram school when he reached fourth grade. He anticipated that the education would be better in this school and looked forward to living in the hostel with his older brother and cousin. However, his mother recalled the transi-tion as being difficult: 'They cry for going to the distant school … they say that the food is not good … it doesn't suit them … they feel they can eat well at home and they can go to school from home.' Balasubramanyam conceded that the food made him sick, although he expressed disappoint-ment at being forced to return to the village school following a bout of appendicitis. His parents want him to move away again to attend a fee-pay-ing, English-language-medium school to benefit from the higher standards of education and his father expressed a willingness to use up to half of the family's meagre income for the fees. His mother explained that they would borrow money or mortgage their house if necessary and regards the pay-ment of fees as ensuring accountability: 'We don't know whether they teach well or not [in government schools] but in private schools we pay the money so they take care.' Their poverty means that the youngest son will only go to private school when Balasubramanyam has completed his education, while the eldest is expected to leave school early to help on the family farm.

Even though parents generally hold strong views on their children's schooling, many have little or no education themselves and therefore have limited understanding of the kinds of knowledge or skills that best promote social advancement in adulthood. Thus the cost-benefit calculations around formal education are extremely precarious. Rural caregivers across diverse contexts articulated only vague ideas about what to expect from their children's schooling and many appeared quite detached from the experience of education more generally. For example, an illiterate mother in Peru explained that the only way she can judge how her children are doing at school is by the volume of red pen marks in their exercise books. Other parents in Peru seemed to be intimidated by teachers who, for instance, reprimand them for not assisting their children with their homework.

Across the wider sample, criticism of specific schools often focuses on the food and facilities rather than the quality of teaching, while the advantages of schooling are described in extremely generalised, idealistic terms, without reference to desired levels of attainment or competencies. For instance, in rural Ethiopia, where few in the parental or grandparental generation have much education, adults talked about schooling merely as ensuring that children are 'smart' or 'wiser' than their elders, preventing early marriage among girls or guaranteeing good employment. Clearly, a paucity of educational experience among adults could in itself be an impetus in education-related child migration inasmuch as parents aspire to give their children opportunities that they themselves lacked.

Sometimes children's preferences also focus more on facilities than pedagogic substance, as can be seen in examples from Patna, a tribal community in Andhra Pradesh. Poor food and hygiene were the most often cited reasons for returning home or changing school hostels in that community. Nevertheless, in many cases, boys and girls have a stronger awareness of the criteria relevant to school choice than do their parents. Several of the children in Patna confirmed that moving away for school was about accessing better-quality teaching and exposure to the wider world, as one 12-year-old girl reasoned:

> [I]f one remains at home all the time it may not be possible to know anything about the outside world. So I want to go out. ... One ought to know about the world outside. So, I want to join a hostel and know much more ... I feel I might be able to live.

4. Social reproduction: interdependence and mutuality

Given the high levels of inter-generational dependence within families and the importance of respect for elders, it would be misleading to claim that school selection by children is a simple manifestation of individual agency. Nonetheless, respondents in the older cohort do repeatedly take the initiative in migration decisions. For example, Alvaro, who is from a village in Andahuaylas, one of the poorest regions in Peru, and has five brothers and sisters, chose to move into a children's home run by a former priest in a nearby town. His reasoning was that this was his only chance of attending a good school given his family's poverty and that living in Andahuaylas would enable him to access the Internet and libraries for homework. By the third round of qualitative data gathering, Alvaro had reached the fifth grade in an agricultural secondary school and was planning to study civil engineering in Lima.

Biritu, who is from Ethiopia's Oromia region and was aged 15 when last interviewed, also took the decision to search for a better school:

> It was me who made up the idea. You know my parents do not go to schools with me for that matter. Then they cannot judge whether I am learning or not. When I evaluated my grades in the past seven grades, I found out that I was not able to sit for the next year national examination because we were not taught very well. I told my parents about this and they agreed with me.

Her mother struggles financially, having raised five children with little support from her husband, who is an alcoholic. Even so, Biritu opted for a private school in a nearby town, where she lives with her older brother, who is studying nursing and helps with her homework and the purchase of school materials.

There are several examples among Young Lives respondents of children migrating to households willing to underwrite their education. Haftey, an orphan from Ethiopia's Tigray region, was raised initially by her grandmother, who is widowed and very poor. The grandmother has had a difficult life, having been unhappily married at the age of nine and going on to bear nine children by her second husband, only two of whom survived. Believing that her lack of 'worldliness' played a significant part in her troubles, she regards her granddaughter's future as contingent upon schooling and decided that Haftey should move to the regional capital to live with an aunt and uncle so that they could bankroll her education. The grandmother observed:

> … it is difficult for me to afford her expenses there. … You know how difficult it is to be orphaned? If she had lost only one parent, that parent would do everything, but I can't. I sent her there because I can't buy her exercise books, can't pay house rent, afford her food ….

In several instances across the sample, children's mobility clearly reinforces mutual relations between generations within extended families. When Buzunesh, a paternal orphan from Oromia in Ethiopia, reached the age of nine, her maternal grandmother fell sick and it was agreed that she should move to live with and care for the old woman. The grandmother described the relocation as part of a reciprocal arrangement decided on by Buzunesh's mother: '… her mother decided that she shall stay here and take care of me until I die. She takes care of me and I take care of her schooling.' Migration also enables children to live in environments that are more conducive to learning, as can be seen from the very different setting of Vietnam. Huu was in eighth grade when his parents became concerned that his enthusiasm for playing video games was detracting from his education. They were both working and did not have the time to watch over him, so it was decided that he should live with his uncle, who agreed to discipline him and ensure that his school grades improved.

Nevertheless, though the young may be decisive about leaving home to expand their educational opportunities, their plans may be thwarted by deep familial responsibilities. When in his early teens, Rajesh, from Andhra Pradesh, had wanted to become a doctor and was studying in a hostel school. But he returned home due to poor health and because his family faced economic difficulties and needed his help on the farm. By the age of 15, he had given up his ambitions to study medicine, rationalising that he wanted to take care of his parents and was in any case unlikely to progress to higher education. Migration arrangements may also break down when expectations of reciprocity are not fulfilled, as when the host household makes unreasonable demands on the child migrant or fails to provide the opportunities that have been promised. In Vietnam, Huu was keen to succeed at school, so remained with his uncle for some time. However, he was required to work in his uncle's shop during term time and began to find high school hard and to fall behind. Eventually, when his brother departed for military service, Huu left school and returned home to support his mother and care for his sick father. This evidence reminds us that schooling can compete with other demands on children's time and that child migration is a complex process often involving reversals and uncertain outcomes.

This section has argued that caregivers and children in the Young Lives study set great store by education, with school selection and school transfers a growing feature of the educational landscape. Inasmuch as local schools are in short supply, or do not meet expectations, school-related child migration may increasingly outweigh considerations of parental proximity or residential fixity. What, then, are the implications for children's social integration and learning, for social reproduction and for educational planning more broadly? These questions are addressed in the concluding section.

5. School-related migration: a challenge to assumptions of residential fixity?

This article has argued that in the four Young Lives countries economic growth, societal transition and service expansion have raised educational aspirations to the point that schooling is, in effect, now perceived to be the sole means of escaping poverty and achieving social mobility. High educational aspirations, stimulated in some settings by wide variation in school accessibility, quality, relevance and social worth, have led to the commoditisation of formal education, which increasingly involves cost-benefit calculations and selection. Extra tuition classes, dual enrolment and school choice all play a part in efforts to maximise children's prospects, with migration for schooling being one consequence.

Child migration has often been problematised in the literature as an expression of disunity within the family and an impediment to children's learning, socialisation and care. Undeniably, this is the case for some children. Then again, from the evidence presented here, it is apparent that children's social and emotional connections to parents and immediate kin are not dependent on physical proximity or remaining within the natal home. Quite the opposite, in reinforcing the domestic economy, serving collective hopes for a better future and consolidating bonds between sending and host households, child relocation can serve to secure children's social integration by buttressing, rather than severing, relations across households and generations of kin. Independent migration may also facilitate children's passage through the life-course by increasing their autonomy and opening up their social and economic horizons. This kind of evidence suggests a normative model of family and child life in contexts of poverty in which young people's mobility should be theorised as core to social reproduction instead of a familial catastrophe. This model has a clear economic logic as well as tremendous social power.

With formal education now a major component in children's repertoire of filial responsibilities, school choice has become a significant motivating factor in their relocation from the natal home, leading to a number of perverse outcomes. First, it has given rise to significant tension between the instrumental and symbolic contributions children make to the household. Serving the immediate material requirements of the domestic economy as well as collective ambitions for the future means that many children straddle their time precariously across school and work, with those who fall behind at school or are forced to leave early often being acutely aware of disappointing their families.

Second, the direct, indirect and opportunity costs of school-related migration sometimes exacerbate rather than alleviate family poverty. Moreover, adults and children with limited educational experience often lack the knowledge and expertise to make informed choices about which schools offer the best returns through future employment and other advantages in adulthood. Third, migratory arrangements can break down, disrupting children's transitions to adulthood. All things considered, despite the current buoyancy of many developing-country economies, school-related migration does not guarantee the kind of adulthood many children and families aspire to, especially given entrenched social hierarchies and restricted labour markets that frequently prevent the poor from accessing good employment. This raises the possibility that, increasingly, child migration for schooling may merely be reproducing or even heightening socio-economic inequalities, rather than mitigating poverty and economic insecurity.

What then, are the responsibilities of education planners? In India, expanding educational opportunities for the poorest and most disadvantaged groups via boarding provision for Scheduled Tribes and seemingly low-cost private options has stimulated educational choice, school mobility and independent child migration. In the other Young Lives countries, the expectation is that children will attend government schools within their localities, at least at primary level. In Ethiopia and Vietnam, there are also wider controls on migration. Therefore, in all cases save India, children accessing schools outside the catchment area is out of alignment with national policy objectives – indeed given the broad policy predisposition against independent child migration, it is surprising that this phenomenon has not attracted more attention as a cause for policy concern. It is important to recognise the part played by education planning in developing countries in encouraging child relocation, inasmuch as it can be attributed to expanding primary schooling and using advocacy and incentives to stimulate demand without at the same time assuring universal coverage, quality and relevance. It is perhaps inevitable that high levels of heterogeneity will encourage the exercise of choice. But school transfers involve risks and costs and choice is not a guarantee of improved outcomes for children or their families.

Undoubtedly, without further expanding supply, raising quality and ensuring curriculum relevance, planning around geographical catchment areas will have very little effect on child mobility. Reaching physically isolated and poorly served communities with more flexible systems, including mobile or distance learning facilities, may have a limited role. But school-related migration among children living in poverty is about social perceptions as much as school realities. This suggests that, ultimately, given the powerful societal processes at play in influencing educational aspirations, the growing commoditisation of schooling and the history of child relocation in many places, school-related child migration is largely beyond the scope of educational, or any other, policy.

Acknowledgements

I am extremely grateful to Emma Wilson for assisting with the research and to Michael Bourdillon, Gina Crivello, Caine Rolleston, Martin Woodhead, the Special Issue editors and two anonymous reviewers for their comments on an earlier draft.

Notes

1. Young Lives is core-funded by the UK Department for International Development and the Netherlands Ministry of Foreign Affairs for the benefit of developing countries, with sub-studies funded by The Bernard van Leer Foun-

dation, the International Development Research Centre, the Oak Foundation and UNICEF.
2. This does not necessarily mean that children who migrate independently are autonomous agents.
3. For details of the methodology see www.younglives.org.uk

References

Akua Anyidoho, N., and P. Ainsworth. 2009. "Child Rural-Rural Migration in West Africa." Workshop Paper: Child and Youth Migration in West Africa: Research Progress and Implications for Policy, University of Sussex and University of Ghana, Accra, June 9–10.

Alber, E. 2003. "Denying Biological Parenthood: Fosterage in Northern Benin." *Ethnos* 68 (4): 487–506. doi:10.1080/0014184032000160532.

Alber, E. 2012. "Schooling or Working? How Family Decision Processes, Children's Agencies and State Policy Influence the Life Paths of Children in Northern Benin." In *African Children at Work: Working and Learning in Growing up for Life*, edited by G. Spittler and M. Bourdillon, 169–194. Berlin: LIT Verlag.

Ansell, N. 2004. "Secondary Schooling and Rural Youth Transitions in Lesotho and Zimbabwe." *Youth and Society* 36 (2): 183–202. doi:10.1177/0044118X 04268376.

Ansell, N., and L. van Blerk. 2004. "Children's Migration as a Household/Family Strategy: Coping with AIDS in Malawi and Lesotho." *Journal of Southern African Studies* 30 (3): 673–690. doi:10.1080/0305707042000254155.

Bano, M. 2007. "Complex Choices: Trends and Motives for Migration within Male and Female Madrasa Students in Pakistan." Workshop Paper: Migration, Education and Socio-Economic Mobility, University of East Anglia, Norwich, November 6–7.

Boonpala, P., and J. Kane. 2001. *Trafficking of Children: The Problem and Responses Worldwide*. Geneva: ILO/IPEC.

Bourdillon, M., D. Levison, W. Myers, and B. White. 2010. *Rights and Wrongs of Children's Work*. New Brunswick, NJ: Rutgers University Press.

Boyden, J., and N. Howard. 2013. "Why Does Child Trafficking Policy Need to Be Reformed? The Moral Economy of Children's Movement in Benin and Ethiopia." *Children's Geographies* 11 (3): 354–368. doi: 10.1080/14733285.2013.817661.

Crivello, G. 2009. "'Becoming Somebody': Youth Transitions through Education and Migration in Peru." *Journal of Youth Studies* 14 (4): 395–411.

Cueto, S., J. Leon, and I. Muñoz. Forthcoming. "Educational Opportunities, Verbal and Math Achievement for Children in Peru: A Longitudinal Model." In *Growing up in Poverty; Findings from Young Lives*, edited by J. Boyden and M. Bourdillon. Basingstoke: Palgrave Macmillan.

Dercon, S., and A. Singh. 2013. "From Nutrition to Aspirations and Self-Efficacy: Gender Bias over Time among Children in Four Countries." *World Development* 45 (May): 31–50. 31–50. doi:10.1016/j.worlddev.2012.12.001.

Dobson, M. 2009. "Unpacking Children in Migration Research." *Children's Geographies* 7 (3): 355–360. doi:10.1080/14733280903024514.

Dougnon, I. 2012. "Migration of Children and Youth in Mali: Global versus Local Discourses." In *African Children at Work; Working and Learning in Growing up for Life*, edited by G. Spittler and M. Bourdillon, 141–168. Zurich and Berlin: LIT Verlag.

Froerer, P. 2011. "Education, Inequality and Social Mobility in Central India." *European Journal of Development Research* 23 (5): 695–711. doi:10.1057/ejdr.2011.43.

Frost, M., and C. Rolleston. 2011. "Improving Education Quality, Equity and Access: A Report on Findings from the Young Lives School Component in Ethiopia." Unpublished, Young Lives.

Galab, S., U. Vennam, A. Komanduri, L. Benny, and A. Georgiadis. Forthcoming. *The Impact of Parental Aspirations on Private School Enrolment: Evidence from Andhra Pradesh, India.* Young Lives Working Paper No. 97. http://www.younglives.org.uk/files/working-papers/yl-wp97_vennam-et-al

Giani, L. 2006. *Migration and Education: Child Migrants in Bangladesh.* University of Sussex, Sussex Migration Working Paper No. 33. www.sussex.ac.uk/migration/documents/mwp33.pdf

Glewwe, P., Q. Chen, and B. Katare. 2012. "What Determines Learning Among Kinh and Ethnic Minority Students in Vietnam? An Analysis of the Round 2 Young Lives Data." Young Lives Working Paper no. 80. Oxford. Accessed September 15, 2012. http://www.younglives.org.uk/files/working-papers/wp80-what-determines-learning-among-kinh-and-ethnic-minority-students-in-vietnam

Hashim, I. 2007. "Independent Child Migration and Education in Ghana." *Development and Change* 38 (5): 911–931. doi:10.1111/dech.2007.38.issue-5.

Hashim, I., and D. Thorsen. 2011. *Child Migration in Africa.* London: Zed Books.

Heissler, K. 2013. "Rethinking 'Trafficking' in Children's Migratory Processes: The Role of Social Networks in Child Labour Migration in Bangladesh." *Children's Geographies* 11 (1): 89–101. doi:10.1080/14733285.2013.743283.

Heissler, K., and C. Porter. Forthcoming. "Know Your Place: Ethiopian Children's Contributions to the Household Economy." *European Journal of Development Research.*

Huijsmans, R. 2008. "Children Working beyond Their Localities: Lao Children Working in Thailand." *Childhood* 15 (3): 331–353. doi:10.1177/0907568208091667.

Iversen, V. 2002. "Autonomy in Child Labor Migrants." *World Development* 30 (5): 817–834. doi:10.1016/S0305-750X(02)00007-4.

James, Z., and M. Woodhead. Forthcoming. "Choosing and Changing Schools in India's Private and Government Sectors." *Oxford Educational Review.*

Le Thuc, D., N. Thang, N. Van Tien, H. Mai Thuy, and T. Vu Thi Thu. 2011. *How Do Children Fare in the New Millennium? Initial Findings from Vietnam, Round 3 Survey Report.* Oxford: Young Lives.

Leinaweaver, J. 2008. *The Circulation of Children: Kinship, Adoption, and Morality in Andean Peru.* Durham, NC: Duke University Press.

Maddox, B. 2010. "Marginal Returns: Re-Thinking Mobility and Educational Benefit in Contexts of Chronic Poverty." *Compare* 40 (2): 213–222.

McKenzie, D., and H. Rapoport. 2006. "Can Migration Reduce Education Attainment? Evidence from Mexico." BREAD Working Paper No. 124.

Murray, H. 2012. "Is School Education Breaking the Cycle of Poverty for Children? Factors Shaping Education Inequalities in Ethiopia, India, Peru and Vietnam." Young Lives Policy Paper 6.

Ni Laoire, C., F. Carpena-Mendez, N. Tyrrell, and A. White. 2010. "Introduction: Childhood and Migration – Mobilities, Homes and Belongings." *Childhood* 17 (2): 155–162. doi:10.1177/0907568210365463.

Ofosu-Kusi, Y., and P. Mizen. 2012. "No Longer Willing to Be Dependent: Young People Moving beyond Learning." In *African Children at Work; Working and*

Learning in Growing up for Life, edited by G. Spittler and M. Bourdillon, 279–302. Zurich and Berlin: LIT Verlag.

Orellana, M., B. Thorne, A. Chee, and W. Lam. 2001. "Transnational Childhoods: The Participation of Children in Processes of Family Migration." *Social Problems* 48 (4): 572–591. doi:10.1525/sp.2001.48.4.572.

Pells, K. 2011. "Poverty and Gender Inequalities: Evidence from Young Lives." Young Lives Policy Paper 3. http://piattaformainfanzia.org/images/items/7341.pdf

Porter, G., K. Hampshire, A. Abane, A. Tanle, K. Esia-Donkoh, R. Obilie Amoako-Sakyi, S. Agblorti, and S. Asiedu Owusu. 2011. "Mobility, Education and Livelihood Trajectories for Young People in Rural Ghana: A Gender Perspective." *Children's Geographies* 9 (3–4): 395–410. doi:10.1080/14733285.2011.590705.

Punch, S. 2007. "Negotiating Migrant Identities: Young People in Bolivia and Argentina." *Children's Geographies* 5 (1–2): 95–112. doi:10.1080/14733280601108213.

Rao, N. 2010a. "Migration, Education and Socio-Economic Mobility." *Compare: A Journal of Comparative and International Education* 40 (2): 137–145.

Rao, N. 2010b. "Aspiring for Distinction: Gendered Educational Choices in an Indian Village." *Compare: A Journal of Comparative and International Education* 40 (2): 167–183. doi:10.1080/03057920903546021.

Robson, E., N. Ansell, U. Huber, W. Gould, and L. van Blerk. 2006. "Young Caregivers in the Context of the HIV/AIDS Pandemic in Sub-Saharan Africa." *Population, Space and Place* 12 (2): 93–111 doi:10.1002/(ISSN)1544-8452.

Rolleston, C., and Z. James. Forthcoming. "Schooling and Cognitive Outcomes from Childhood to Youth: A Longitudinal Analysis." In *Growing up in Poverty; Findings from Young Lives*, edited by J. Boyden and M. Bourdillon. Basingstoke: Palgrave Macmillan.

Schaffer, R. 1999. *Social Development*. Oxford: Blackwell.

Serra, R. 2009. "Child Fostering in Africa: When Labor and Schooling Motives May Coexist." *Journal of Development Economics* 88 (1): 1–184.

Smita, S. 2008. "Distress Seasonal Migration and Its Impact on Children's Education." Create Pathways to Access, Research Monograph No. 28. http://www.create-rpc.org/pdf_documents/PTA28.pdf

Spittler, G., and M. Bourdillon, eds. 2012. *African Children at Work; Working and Learning in Growing up for Life*. Zurich and Berlin: LIT Verlag.

Streuli, N., U. Vennam, and M. Woodhead. 2011. "Increasing Choice or Inequality? Pathways through Early Education in Andhra Pradesh, India." Working Papers in Early Child Development 58. The Hague: Bernard van Leer Foundation.

van Blerk, L. 2005. "Negotiating Spatial Identities: Mobile Perspectives on Street Life in Uganda." *Children's Geographies* 3 (1): 5–21. doi:10.1080/14733280500037091.

Vu, H. Forthcoming. "Ethnic Minority Children's and Adults' Perceptions and Experiences of Schooling in Vietnam: A Case Study of the Cham H'roi." In *Growing up in Poverty; Findings from Young Lives*, edited by J. Boyden and M. Bourdillon. Basingstoke: Palgrave Macmillan.

Whitehead, A., I. Hashim, and V. Iversen. 2007. "Child Migration, Child Agency and Inter-Generational Relations in Africa and South Asia." Working Paper T24, Working Paper Series, Migration DRC, Brighton. http://www.childmigration.net/MigrationDRC_Whitehead_Hashim_Iversen_07

Woldehanna, T., R. Gudisa, Y. Tafere, and A. Pankhurst. 2011. "Understanding Changes in the Lives of Poor Children: Initial Findings from Ethiopia." Round 3 Survey Report, Young Lives.

Woodhead, M., and N. Streuli. 2013. "Early Education for All: Is There a Role for the Private Sector?" In *Handbook of Early Child Development: Translating Research to Global Policy*, edited by P. Britto, P. Engle, and C. Super, 308–328. New York: Oxford University Press.

Zimmerman, F. 2003. "Cinderella Goes to School: The Effects of Child Fostering on School Enrollment in South Africa." *The Journal of Human Resources* 38 (3): 557–590. doi:10.2307/1558768.

Does mobility have to mean being hard to reach? Mobile pastoralists and education's 'terms of inclusion'

Caroline Dyer

Centre for Development Studies, University of Leeds, Leeds, UK

Nomadic groups are highly discriminated against in access to education services, and the 2010 Education For All Global Monitoring Report demanded urgent action to address their education deprivation. Mobile pastoralists, particularly, appear to be falling beyond the remit of migration studies in education, although they are among the most mobile people in the world. Pastoralists' education inclusion has been promoted by models of provision across the 'mainstream', 'alternative' and Open Learning traditions, but examples from around the world show that each broad approach comes with identifiable 'terms of inclusion' that, in different ways, reproduce and/or challenge pastoralists' marginalisation. Achieving political commitment to addressing the scale and extent of pastoralists' education deprivation is not unimaginable, but contingent on significant reappraisal of mobility as a livelihood strategy and of the legitimacy of pastoralism as a sustainable contemporary livelihood.

Introduction

Policy discourses within the Education For All (EFA) movement and Millennium Development Goals (MDG) regime articulate an increasing concern over those who remain excluded from formal education. Reflecting this concern, the 2010 EFA Global Monitoring Report (GMR) focused specifically on 'Reaching the Marginalised', pointing out that 'marginalization in education is a form of acute and persistent disadvantage rooted in underlying social inequalities' (UNESCO 2010, 135). The GMR opted to avoid debating definitions of marginalisation, on the grounds that doing so 'can sometimes obscure the political and ethical imperative to combat [it]' and cited, in favour of this stance, Amartya Sen's view that 'What moves us ... is not the realisation that the world falls short of being completely just ... but that there are clearly remediable injustices around us which we want to eliminate' (Sen 2009, vii, cited in UNESCO 2010, 135). Holding up education marginalisation as a 'stark example of "clearly remediable injustice"', it argued that 'Removing that injustice should be at the centre of the national and international Education for All agendas' (UNESCO 2010, 135).

Twenty years before the publication of that GMR, Article 3 of the 1990 World Declaration on Education For All had identified nomads specifically as one of several groups who are discriminated against in access to education services, and demanded 'an active commitment' to removing educational disparities (WDEFA 1990). Nomadic groups are again identified, in the 2010 GMR, as continuing to face extreme educational disadvantage, and the need for 'urgent action' is underlined (UNESCO 2010). Policy discourses aiming to tackle the now increasingly visible exclusion of nomads now recognise them as among those who are 'hard to reach'. Nevertheless, this homogenising categorisation, imposed on extreme heterogeneity (even among nomadic groups), has gained a considerable hold in the global education policy arena – as the 2010 GMR's title illustrates. There is in this label an inherently reassuring vision of a future in which the injustice of education deprivation has been overcome, but it is unlikely that very significant progress can be made without deconstructing the nature of injustice that perpetuates marginalisation for particular groups. Sen's (2009) argument is not that we argue for identifying the ideal conditions of a perfectly just society – on which there can be no agreement – but, instead, we should focus on people's lives and improve our ability to 'make decisions about justice-enhancing and justice-reducing responses to particular problems' (Arjona et al. 2012, 156). We need to ask, then, whether there is something particular about *nomads* and education marginalisation and what perspectives on education deprivation lie behind strategies for education inclusion for these mobile people.

This paper explores these issues in relation to mobile pastoralists, a particular 'nomadic' group who – paradoxically, considering how mobile they are – remain outside the frame of migration studies in education. Pastoralists have been marginalised by unsympathetic 'governmentality' (African Union Commission 2010; Morton 2010) and subjected to many cumulative failures of development policies. Here, I use a livelihoods-orientated analysis (Scoones 2009) to identify the 'terms of inclusion' of strategies used around the world that have aimed to address pastoralists' education deprivation. I derive this analytical concept from studies of adverse incorporation and social exclusion (cf. du Toit 2005; Hickey and du Toit 2007; [see Dyer (2012) for more detail and application in Western India]) and use it here as a heuristic device to highlight the global dimensions of unjust institutional arrangements in education for mobile pastoralists, and to identify 'ways of judging' (Sen 2009, ix) the injustice they represent to them.

This paper falls into four sections. The first provides an overview of pastoralist populations around the world, explains why the term 'nomad' is analytically unhelpful and gives a sense of global progress towards pastoralists' inclusion in formal schooling. The second focuses on mobility as a misunderstood pastoralist livelihood strategy, implicated in a historically negative framing of pastoralism that has helped to *create* a trajectory of the disadvantage to which the 2010 GMR refers, which is not the same as being 'hard to reach'. Drawing on the 'mobility' paradigm of pastoralist studies, it builds the more accurate understandings needed to respond to the EFA call for 'urgent action'. The third section discusses 'education deprivation' with reference to three forms of education service provision, which broadly comprise the 'mainstream', the 'alternative' and Open and Distance Learning. The conclusion reflects on the challenges of crafting appropriate responses to pastoralists' education deprivation and sustainable livelihood challenges in the post-2015 era.

1. Pastoralists: a global overview

Nomads[1] comprise millions of people around the world who live on land and water and deploy spatial mobility as a strategy by which to access the resources they require to sustain their livelihood. They include: foragers, or hunter-gatherers – the Kalahari bushmen, the Spinifex or Pila Nguru people in the Great Victoria Desert of Western Australia and the Batak of Northern Palawan in Western Philippines[2]; 'peripatetic' people (Rao and Casimir 2003), who generally offer specialised services to sedentary, or, indeed, other nomadic people, such as itinerant pot menders in India, Gypsy and Travelling groups in the UK and performance artists such as snake charmers in India, Sri Lanka and Bangladesh; the sea nomads of Indonesia or fisherfolk of Nigeria; and pastoralists – mobile animal husbanders – on whom this paper focuses.

Pastoralism is itself a categorisation that is 'fuzzy' and excites controversy (cf. Rao and Casimir 2003). Broadly speaking, mobile pastoralists[3] are people who raise livestock and move them to pastures, sustaining themselves mostly – but rarely entirely – from the domestic consumption or sale/ exchange of animals and/or their products. Pastoralism makes productive use of the natural resources available in the extreme climatic conditions of the world's fragile drylands. Pastoralist activities are remarkably widespread, covering about a quarter of the earth's surface spread across north and sub-Saharan Africa, south and central Asia, the circumpolar region, the middle East, northern and southern Europe and Latin America (Blench 2001). Geographic diversity is accompanied by wide variety in socio-economic organisation and in the wider history, socio-political economy and ecology of the specific livelihood context.

Globally, estimates of pastoralist population are, at best, speculative. Carr-Hill (2012) points out how data gathering instruments typically 'omit *by design*' (italics in original) mobile, nomadic or pastoralist populations. They are often absent when surveys are carried out and are rarely captured in census counts, an omission then perpetuated in sector-specific household sample surveys, which generally base their sampling frame on census data. Definitional ambiguities, in turn, can 'easily double or half the numbers' (de Weijer 2005, 6). The struggle over population counts is well illustrated in the widely cited figures provided by the UN's Food and Agriculture Organisation, which suggest that there are between 100 and 200 million pastoralists worldwide (FAO 2003). These 'gaps in the administrative data' (Carr-Hill 2012) are pointed out in the 2010 GMR, which notes the absence of adequate, accurate evidence as to actual numbers in and out of schooling and alludes to their inconsistent visibility. This is itself part of a cycle of marginalisation in public policies, which rely on population counts to formulate priorities and allocate resources.

While it raised the profile of pastoralists in general, the 2010 GMR's focus was firmly on Africa. There is a relatively rich body of scholarship on pastoralism in Africa (and to a lesser extent the Middle East [see Chatty 2006b]), reflecting a long-standing concern – addressed in different ways by governments, donor agencies and non-governmental organisations (NGOs) – with pastoralism there and the currently high profile of drought and insecurity in the region (although, in general, a discourse of pastoralism in crisis is not new [see Blench 2001]). There has been a surprising neglect of pastoralism in South Asia (Rao and Casimiir 2003). This is gradually being addressed (cf. Sharma, Köhler-Rollefson, and Morton 2003; Agrawal and Saberwal 2004), but is something of a paradox given that this region is home to the world's largest and most diverse nomadic population in general, among whom millions are pastoralists. In India, for example, pastoralists number at least six million people, both Hindu and Muslim: some practise 'vertical' mobility between winter and summer pastures in the Himalayas, herding yaks, cattle, sheep and goats (Rao and Casimir 2003; Rao 2006), while across western and central India and on towards the South, 'horizontal' mobility takes place, with sheep, cattle, goats, camels – and even ducks (Nambi 2001).

The extent of pastoralists' education deprivation is very poorly documented and in official discourses tends to be narrowly interpreted as lack of formal (primary) schooling. Globally, Carr-Hill (2012) estimates that in EFA Fast Track Initiative countries, there are about 4.3 million uncounted, out-of-school pastoralist children; this rises to 21.8 million globally. His 2005 study of six countries in the Horn of Africa found the percentage of school-age children in pastoralist populations then going to school varied between 11% and 39% (Carr-Hill 2006). The 2010 GMR captures statistics for six African countries with high pastoralist populations and shows that, compared with country averages, young pastoralist adults' record of formal education tends to be one of severely limited initial enrolment and very poor retention (see Ruto, Ongwenyi, and Mugo [2009] for further detail). This suggests a need to look beyond an idea of 'hard to reach' to a global trend of marginalisation and education deprivation that is gradually becoming evidenced (see overviews in Krätli 2001; Dyer 2006; MoESTK/UNICEF 2006; Danaher, Kenny, and Leder 2009) and clearly demands exploration.

2. Mobilities, livelihoods and education deprivation

Pastoralists appear a contradiction to development policy narratives and their overarching concern with agendas of modernity, growth and productivity (Scott 1998; Krätli 2001; Andreasson 2006). In post-colonial contexts, a colonial association of mobility with criminality casts a long shadow over mobility, in general, as uncivilised and morally inferior to a sedentary lifestyle (cf. Kenny and Danaher 2009). Pastoralist practices, specifically, are interpreted as archaic, backward, culture-bound, ecologically damaging, insufficiently productive and generally irrational in the pursuit of state-building (Scott 1998; Krätli 2001; Krätli and Dyer 2009). Typically, 'State agents consider nomads in general as belligerent, difficult to control, and see their continuous movement much more as a sort of offence to the requirements of any *modern* state and its *rational* administration than as a quest for water and pasture' (Klute 1996, 3, italics added, see also Morton 2010). The 'myths of pastoralism' that feed this 'governmentality' are widespread and readily identifiable (see Table 1).

Reflecting such sentiments, modernising policy discourses tend to frame pastoralism as deservedly obsolescent, suggesting a key role for formal education in modernising (i.e., changing, civilising and sedentarising) pastoral-

Table 1. The World Initiative for Sustainable Pastoralism summary of 10 misconceptions about pastoralism.

1. Nomadic pastoralism is an archaic form of production, whose time has passed.
2. Mobility is inherently backward, unnecessary, chaotic and disruptive.
3. Most rangelands are degraded as a result of pastoral over-grazing.
4. Pastoralists do not take care of the land because of the Tragedy of the Commons.
5. African pastoralists do not sell their animals; they prefer to hoard them, admire them and compose poems to them.
6. Pastoralists contribute little to national economic activity.
7. Pastoralism has very low productivity. Sedentary cattle raising is more productive than mobile systems.
8. Pastoral techniques are archaic: modern scientific methods need to be introduced.
9. Pastoralists need to settle to benefit from services.
10. All pastoralists are rich; alternatively, all pastoralists are poor and food insecure.

Source: UNDP (2003)/World Initiative for Sustainable Pastoralism.

ists. Let me illustrate this with Ethiopia's Pastoralist Area Strategy (PEAS nd), which claims that the 'down-trodden economic status of pastoralists that is mainly based on backward animal rearing practices and severely limits their capacity to support the education system financially and materially' is one of the 'numerous bottlenecks that hinder the expansion of quality education in pastoralist areas'. It goes on to demonstrate its interpretation of barriers to accessing formal education by stressing the need to, 'Devise strategies that diminish the interference of child labour on the education of pastoralist children such as making the time of learning flexible enough to be determined by parents themselves and taking education to the village where children reside'. Here we see poverty, backwardness, resistance, labouring children (and an assumption of sedentary village living), all of which can be 'cured' by education, subject to minor adaptations of the education system. This is not an unusual perspective (Dyer [2014] gives other examples).

An alternative to this deficit framing emerges from the 'mobility paradigm' of pastoralism studies (Scoones 1995; IIED 2009; Mortimore et al. 2009), which focuses on pastoralists' skilful management of uncertainty and risk in arid land ecosystems. It argues for pastoralism as a sophisticated, environmentally friendly livelihood (ECHO 2009) that requires social, economic and political constraints to be lifted to achieve its full potential for sustainability (Niamir-Fuller 1990). Contrary to an idea of wilful wandering, mobility is a livelihood strategy that pastoralists use, along with herd formation and division of labour (Galaty and Johnston 1990, 4), to access fleeting, dispersed and uncertain supplies of high-quality nutrition for livestock. Such mobility typically involves a wide range of spatial movements, where neither distance, frequency nor pattern is arbitrary or fixed. It is essential to maintaining pastoralist animals, which are dynamic, (re-)productive assets, at or above the critical asset 'threshold' that makes pastoralism a sustainable livelihood. Learning to manage a mobile herd is a lengthy process of on-the-job training, or 'legitimate peripheral participation' (Lave and Wenger 1991), and pastoralist children are trained to carry out responsible independent roles on behalf of the collective from an age of approximately seven (cf. Rao 2006). This work is prone to being labelled a form of child labour that prevents children from being able to enrol in school, but it is a form of intensive, situated education for which formal education offers no substitute, although it has the potential to add value and different, complementary skills.

In the education sector, mobility in isolation has been the dominant explanation of why pastoralists are 'hard to reach' (and retain). A descriptive typology of movement to categorise whole population groups of pastoralists – as *nomadic, semi-nomadic, transhumant* (e.g. Woldemichael 1995; Tahir 1997; Carr-Hill 2006) – obfuscates, however, through oversimplification. It neglects the 'animal factor' (Galaty and Johnston 1990, 22) that provides the underlying rationale for mobility, reifying the 'nomadic factor' (22) yet overlooking its co-dependence on strategies of herd formation and labour distribution and the critical role of situated learning to livelihood sustainability. A holistic livelihood perspective, in contrast, draws to attention the prior existence of this form of education. From this perspective, if pastoralism is to be a sustainable livelihood in future, socially just remedial action to address pastoralists' 'education deprivation' will envisage formalised education as *complementary to*, rather than *in competition with*, situated livelihood learning.

Furthermore, combinations of mobility, herd formation and labour distribution vary widely among contemporary pastoralist 'households'. This has important implications for education provision. Many households combine mobile livestock keeping with other occupations, which allows diversification of income-generating strategies and changes patterns of labour absorption. This is typically done by household splitting. In East Africa, for example, some pastoralists and their animals are fully mobile, but larger numbers establish a base camp or settlement with 'satellite' herding camps (Little et al. 2008). All animals move but only select family members, most likely younger men, move with them, leaving other members free to supplement pastoral incomes through milk sales, casual labour, petty trade, farming and/or schooling. Among the Rabaris of Kutch in Western India, mostly men now migrate with animals, while many women and children have sedentarised (Dyer 2012) and a Kenyan Orma family that comprises two or more households may split to allow one (or more) to sedentarise while the other(s) remains mobile (Pattison 2011, 255).

Pastoralism does not contain the seeds of its own ruin, as the deficit discourse assumes, but becomes a vulnerable livelihood when the mobility on which pastoralist systems depend is curtailed. Almost everywhere in the world, this mobility is ever more constrained by changing land management and tenure systems (Nori 2007). Education must engage with this trend. Pastoralists do not necessarily want to stop being pastoralists when this is a viable livelihood, and particularly in contexts where it is uniquely appropriate and alternatives are unlikely, but few nowadays argue against the benefit to them of skills related to using the written word, interpreting information and being able to assert themselves, or against the status advantage associated with being 'educated'. These forms of learning are associated with the external provision of which so many pastoralists are deprived (GMR 2010).

3. Forms of education provision for pastoralists and their terms of inclusion

How, then, do these competing perspectives on mobility and livelihood legitimacy map onto education service provision? The institutional arrangements put into place over the years to respond to the challenges of educating pastoralist children have taken three broad forms. Each has specific 'terms of inclusion' for pastoralist households to consider, and all reflect difficulties in making substantial progress towards rectifying the 'remediable injustice' of education deprivation. Even the more progressive 'solutions' I will discuss carry identifiable markers of, and perpetuate, marginalisation.

Formal education and inclusion in the 'mainstream'

Under the MDG regime, there has been a general emphasis on school access (Lewin and Sabates 2011). Expanding the network of fixed-place, state-run primary schools to consolidate and extend their availability is understood to facilitate universal access and education inclusion by enhancing schools' physical proximity for learners. Such provision is, in the policy gaze, understood to be 'mainstream' and includes a standard sedentary response to extending provision to mobile pastoralist learners: boarding schools.

Infrastructural development in zones conducive to pastoralism has, nevertheless, rarely seen adequate investment. Where population densities are low, learners are scattered, and economies of scale are difficult to achieve, policy norms have rarely succeeded in ensuring that primary schools are available and/or consistently meet stipulated quality thresholds. These are often also areas where conflict is ongoing and/or a sudden escalation of violence is likely (IGAD 2007). Expanding school systems are already challenged to provide and retain adequate numbers of well-trained teachers (Murphy and Wolfenden 2013) – all the more so in the harsh conditions where pastoralism thrives. Selecting teachers from pastoralist backgrounds is an obvious strategy but since few pastoralists have been able to access even initial primary education, very few attain eligibility for teacher education programmes (McCaffery et al. 2006). This is particularly true for women (cf. Sanou and Aikman 2005) and how to generate a pool of female teachers is a critical consideration for pastoralist communities everywhere.

While sparsity of provision is a consideration, as are other infrastructural and staffing challenges that shape quality dimensions in general, making schools physically available does not necessarily ensure favourable terms of inclusion for pastoralists. The more fundamental justice challenge is mainstream schooling's conflict with their livelihood prerequisites. Schools have extreme difficulty in accommodating patterns of learner attendance that do not adhere to everyday, taken-for-granted, institutional norms, such as fixed school calendars and timetables, a set annual enrolment point, cohort-based teaching and progression on an annual cycle, often linked to examination success. These typical features of mass public school systems impose terms of inclusion that depend on pastoralist households' capacity and/or willingness to adjust their production strategies in order to use this service without later negative impact on livelihood security. Typically, if household splitting is avoided, access comes on the term of curtailing mobility so the whole family and their animals can remain near a fixed-place school. This, if accepted, may decrease animal nutrition, health and (re)productivity, while potentially also precipitating over-grazing in a concentrated area (and making the third 'myth' of Table 1 a more likely reality), meaning that education inclusion can increase vulnerability to wealth decumulation and impoverishment as a pastoralist. This risk may, nevertheless, be assessed against the prospects of school inclusion leading to employability in the non-pastoralist sector and 'future proofing' the family, particularly when pressures on pastoralism show little sign of diminishing.

Where household splitting is practised to meet the terms of inclusion imposed by institutional norms of this nature, it can facilitate school enrolment, but tends to do so unevenly because of prevailing gendered patterns of labour distribution. Boys assigned to go with herds are unlikely ever to attend school but, with those important exceptions, splitting tends to favour boys' enrolment, as boys will have comparatively few – if any – herding duties within a settled household, while girls see little reduction in the household tasks to which they are likely to be assigned.

Research on school access has found a strong association between access to schooling and household wealth: *lack* of household wealth is generally the most powerful determinant of education exclusion (Lewin and Sabates 2011). The relationship between accessing formal education and pastoralist wealth dynamics is very slimly evidenced but points towards divergent trends, consistent with the pastoralist livelihood management strategies laid out above. Where higher-wealth families have larger animal holdings and, accordingly, higher household labour and mobility requirements, their children may be less likely to be enrolled (see Pattison 2011). Less wealthy families, with lower production levels, probably linked to reduced household mobility, generate a labour surplus. This, if it cannot be absorbed within pastoralism (since decumulation wealth dynamics affect the larger community), becomes available for other activity – such as schooling (Pattison 2011; see also Dyer 2012). Among the Harasiis in Oman, however, the wealthiest families hire less wealthy pastoralists (from Balochistan) to tend their animals (Chatty, personal communication May 2012).

How households respond to the livelihood implications of schooling's terms of inclusion is also contingent upon their assessments of schooling's processes and likely outcomes, which links to matters of quality and the availability of work/fit between schooling and work. The difficulties so many schools have in delivering even basic reading and writing skills or ensuring teacher presence (e.g. papers in Dyer 2013) are realities that may well belie both the hopes vested in schooling and efforts made to meet its terms of inclusion. An illustrative example is Kutch, in Western India, where rapid dispossession from the land has precipitated unprecedented pastoralist take-up of formal schooling. Reflecting on what his fellow Rabaris have been experiencing since 2001 as they split households, adjust flock size and management and reduce household income in order to enrol their children in state-run, fixed-place day schools (Dyer 2012), this respondent summarised experience with much wider resonance:

> They had 100 animals now they have cut it down to 50. They reduced the number of animals so the men could still look after the animals and the women have come back here to educate their children. They help each other out and keep animals together [i.e., merge individual household's flocks], helping each other. That's how they are managing and women have come back to educate children but education here is very bad. They are trying to be educated, wasting their time and education is not good here. (Verabhai Rabari, personal communication, December 2009)

Once the means of production (animals) have been ceded, and if schooling fails them, extreme poverty is more likely to be found among 'exited' pastoralists than it is among those who sustain their pastoralist livelihood (Little et al. 2008; see also Greany's [2012] study of Karimojong young people in Kampala slums).

Recognising at least some of the difficulties for pastoralists in accessing fixed-place day schools, state authorities have established boarding schools for pastoralists in a wide range of contexts, including Mongolia, Kenya, Nigeria, Oman and Iran (see chapters in Dyer 2006). Perhaps because, more than the day schools discussed above, boarding schools entirely remove children from situated learning for a high proportion of the annual cycle, they even more sharply illustrate how intertwined are perceptions of the legitimacy of pastoralism and the instrumental use of schooling to educate children out of pastoralism. Mongolia is an excellent case in point. Until it transitioned to the market economy in the 1990s, pastoralists, who represented almost 50% of the population, were integral to Mongolia's identity and economy and the state invested extensively in supporting pastoralism (Krätli 2001). Transition saw a reduction in state-provided services, investment and governance that undermined the nationwide boarding school network (Steiner-Khamsi and Stolpe 2005; Demberel and Penn 2006). Collectives of animal herders were disbanded by privatisation of livestock and this, in turn, increased demand for children to contribute their labour to the household, leaving the challenge with which Mongolia is now grappling (familiar from other contexts) of a mismatch between the nature, quality and extent of formal education provision, and demand.

In other contexts, Shahbazi's (2006) account of his experience in Iran's famous tent boarding schools, and Chatty's (2006a) account from Oman of the state-initiated boarding school for Harasiis pastoralists, both examine state attempts to use boarding schools instrumentally to incorporate pastoralists. In both these cases, mutual engagement and negotiation over acceptable terms of inclusion is evident, but resistance to incorporation as an overarching term of education inclusion is not inevitable. Much depends on the context and pastoralist assessments of the future viability of their livelihood. In Kutch, for example, the pace and onslaught of change since economic liberalisation in 1991 has rapidly undermined land and natural resource availability. Pastoralist youths discussing their hopes of 'progress' through formal education offered in 2009 a narrative of pastoralism as backward and menial that closely mirrors generic state narratives of modernity, progress and development, exemplified in this respondent's view:

> My father is … breaking his bones on the hard work of grazing animals. He has been doing this for the last 40 years and his forefathers did it before him. … I am working very hard now and I want to move ahead; I want to study and I want to liberate my father and mother from this roaming business. I want to study and work really hard so that my family can be relieved from it. My father didn't get any education so he joined this business and he carried on with it till now. When I study and get a job, I will give my father and mother peace. … I want to free them from this body breaking, hard working business. (Focus-group-discussion, Year 12 Rabari boys, December 2009)

'Alternative' basic education: inclusion on more favourable terms?

Formal schooling's terms of inclusion tend to position pastoralism and formal education at odds with one another, and to set those who accept them on a trajectory out of pastoralism – which may, indeed, be a reason for acceptance. The terms of inclusion of alternative basic education (ABE), in contrast, are framed by the premise that pastoralism is legitimate, that education within this livelihood is a right and should complement situated livelihood learning and, thus, that service provision needs to be flexible and probably move to, or with, mobile learners. Teacher recruitment can prioritise the criteria of being 'local' and having relevant language skills over formal qualifications, the curriculum can be adapted for content and delivery timing that fit local needs, and provision can take various physical forms – for example bus, boat, tent, box on a camel. Alternative basic education for pastoralists has attracted extensive external agency support, often in partnership with the host state and taking the form of mobile provision. In Sudan, Unicef sponsorship in the mid-1990s helped establish some 200 mobile schools; Kenya has over 50; in Karamoja, Uganda, the Alternative Basic Education collaboration between Save the Children Norway and the Uganda Ministry of Education introduced in 2009 about 15 mobile schools and an Oxfam-supported sister programme in Turkana, Kenya (ABET) runs about 30 (Oxfam 2009) (summaries and full references in Dyer 2014).

Mobile schools, nevertheless, are subject to complex logistics. Assuring the sustained availability of a viable concentration of learners is difficult, since the combinations of causes that can bring groups of pastoralist learners together are transient and unpredictable, influenced by factors such as seasonal scarcity or plenty, community organisation, deteriorating security and so on. Such contingencies are likely to remain a constitutive factor of service provision in pastoralist zones. In Kenya's northern grazing areas, for example, mobile camel-back schools set up in 2008 by the local community-based organisation Frontier Indigenous Network to serve Somali pastoralists were forced by extended drought to close in 2011. Some pastoralists crossed the border to Somalia in search of pasture and water to save their livestock, while others, including the two teachers, headed for urban areas (http://www.grassrootsonline.org/).

Sustaining literacy abilities once learned (difficult in physical environments of this nature) can be resolved to some extent by mobile book-lending services. Kenya's National Library Service, supported by BookAid International (http://www.bookaid.org/our-work/where-we-work/kenya/camel-library-service/), runs three camel libraries carrying about 200 books. Save the Children UK and a Somali NGO have developed a camel library (Berry 2010) for the Somali region, which, fully operational from 2010, visits 10 communities monthly, allowing about 500 children to benefit. The Library follows a shorter route than planned because the distances are so great that insufficient time could be spent at each stop, and has faced challenges of supplying suitable, relevant materials in Somali and of sufficiently durable production quality. This initiative aims to address Ethiopia's 2010 Early Grade Reading Assessments finding that 34% of grade 2 children were unable to read a single word of the test reading passage (Akyeampong et al. 2013).

Community-based schools offer terms of inclusion that complement socialisation as a pastoralist by providing small children with formalised education within the domestic sphere (Bangsbo 2008). The Swedish Committee for Afghanistan (http://www.swedishcommittee.org/our-work/education) has provided gender-segregated schools in tents for Kuchi pastoralists, which are located within temporary settlements, staffed by community members and deliver instruction in Pashto. These have shown remarkable success in generating parental interest and enrolling girls – by 2010, almost 50% of enrolled Kuchi children were female. Another approach combines religious education, provided within the community, with secular inputs offered by external providers. Education for Marginalized Communities in Kenya runs mobile schools for 5–14-year-old Somali pastoralists in Wajir District. Schools combine learning basic literacy and numeracy skills with learning Muslim religious traditions, via the Somali Quranic School, or 'dugsi' (USAID 2012). Each comprises basic learning equipment and two camels and has a 'dugsi' and a secular teacher, the latter selected by the community and trained by the donor/state partnership. Children learn the Qu'ran for two years, typically attending a 'dugsi' class for six to seven hours each day, while also taking care of younger siblings and herding livestock. The secular curriculum wraps around these commitments, offering basic literacy and numeracy for two hours, morning and evening. By March 2012, three mobile schools were serving some 80 children, including 28 girls, and 14 children had transitioned to a nearby boarding school to complete the primary stage (USAID 2012).

In high-altitude herding areas of Tibet, local Buddhist lamas continue their tradition as educators by running small community schools, which are often funded through charitable organisations in foreign countries, reflecting international concern with the future of Tibet and forced sedentarisation of pastoralists by the Chinese government. Bangsbo (2008) remarks on parental reluctance to send small children, especially girls, to the other form of available education – state boarding schools. Parents' reasoning is consistent with experience elsewhere: boarding schools require household splitting and they disseminate through the formal and informal curricula and language of instruction political/socialising messages that families wish to resist. The community schools enjoy relative freedom from the rules governing state schools but, consistent with ABE's problem of accreditation, are not authorised to provide certificates of graduation. Transition into higher education levels remains problematic and, amid disappointment that elementary-level education does not result in a good job, Bangsbo (2008) reports that parental aspiration for higher levels of education remains low.

Alternative basic education provision derives legitimacy from its accountability and acceptability to pastoralist learners, which positively influences the terms of inclusion it offers. It is undemanding in relation to material and capital construction costs, and aims to recognise and complement pastoralism as a livelihood, rather than provide an exit route from it[4]. Experience from Kenya (Pattison 2011), Afghanistan and Tibet (Bangsbo 2008) suggests that, for girls in particular, ABE's physical proximity, sensitivity to cultural mores, curricular independence and selection of teachers combine to offer highly favourable terms of education inclusion. Alternative basic education exploits the 'space' of the margin (Devereux 2010) – both symbolically and practically it represents resistance to the adverse incorporation of pastoralism by offering externally provided education that is orientated towards providing skills and knowledge to help sustain pastoralism. Potentially, through this affirmation, ABE offers opportunity to develop voice and engage with the wider politics of pastoralist (mis)representation and marginalisation. In all these respects, ABE admirably addresses the remediable injustice of education deprivation.

The space of the margin can be interpreted positively, as I have just done, but conversely, some of ABE's terms of inclusion are problematic from a social justice perspective. Alternative basic education is generally an offer of no more than basic education and unlikely to furnish the certification offered by 'mainstream' schooling. Learners wishing to progress beyond basic education and/or acquire certification need then to turn to formal provision and negotiate the associated terms of inclusion discussed above. A term of inclusion associated with ABE is almost certainly the forgoing of the symbolic power and cultural capital that pastoralists themselves, and others, associate with formal education provision; and in India, this has been linked to non-acceptance of a mobile provision (Dyer 2008, 2012). Relying on 'alternative' provision to redress the 'clearly remediable injustice' of education deprivation for marginalised groups is, in relation to this term of inclusion, insufficient if such education does not carry equivalent social, symbolic status.

Open and distance learning: inclusion in a deeper, broader, 'mainstream'?

Open and distance learning (ODL) is a third, overarching approach to addressing mobile pastoralists' education deprivation. Open and distance learning, which offers learners the opportunity to study in their own environment, at their own pace, with appropriate support (Perraton 2007), has an intrinsic flexibility that enables it in principle to respond to learners, wherever and whoever they are, independently of classrooms (Krätli and Dyer 2009). It has the capacity to address mobile pastoralists' education deprivation by offering accredited formal education, delivered within a livelihood context and as a complement to situated learning. In developing country contexts, however, ODL is more familiar as an auxiliary input to enhance delivery of the school curriculum and/or support teachers in resource-constrained formal systems. Its promise for marginalised pastoralist learners lies in the possibility of integrating ODL as a delivery strategy within a broadened concept of a formal education system – making the notion of 'hard to reach' learners superfluous.

The full potential of this approach is demonstrated by Australia's School of the Air (SoA) for outback children (http://australia.gov.au/about-australia/australian-story/school-of-the-air). By 2005, 16 SoAs offered a network covering more than 1.5 million km^2 and a programme that includes secondary students and adult education courses. Each SoA covers the same curriculum as any other school in the state, tailored to an individual student as far as possible, and from its early beginnings with two-way radios, Internet-based technology now facilitates real-time interactive learning. Its estimated cost is, however, twice that of school-based provision[5].

In Kenya in 2010, the Ministries of Education and of Development of the Northern Arid and Semi-Arid Lands (MDNKOAL) developed a radio-based strategy for the 'hard to reach' (MDNKOAL 2010) in pursuit of national policy objectives for nomadic education (MoESTK 2010). Largely bypassing face-to-face delivery, it seeks to ensure that pastoralist learners can access, with no constraints, the formal school curriculum, which is converted into units appropriate for distance delivery and offered as a combination of pre-recorded lessons, available on a card to listen to at any time, print materials and radio broadcasts addressing learner questions and educational issues. Support to learners is mobile, supplemented by sedentary key points at radio stations that mobile pastoralists can access when convenient. The strategy offers a radical change of delivery approach in a broadened notion of 'mainstream' provision and demonstrates political engagement with the need to invest energy, resources and imagination in taking action[6]. This is a promising but still thin version of addressing pastoralists' education deprivation. It focuses on the terms of inclusion relating to access to formal education opportunity within a mobile livelihood and successfully improves several of those, but does not challenge the appropriateness of existing national curricular content for pastoralist learners. A response more deeply focused on social justice would require to build beyond a (successful but) largely technicist approach to equal access and education inclusion and engage with the pressing question of the relevance of the national curriculum to pastoralists' livelihood sustainability.

Conclusion

From the social justice perspective that Sen (2009) espouses, to which the 2010 GMR refers, and with which I began, it is evident that addressing the 'clearly remedial injustice' of pastoralists' education deprivation is a multifaceted challenge of far greater scope and political complexity than the 'hard to reach' label suggests. While there can be no disputing the need for urgent action, it is essential to recognise that this deprivation reflects long-standing social discrimination rooted in the contested legitimacy of a mobile pastoralist livelihood. A strong and relevant response to this injustice cannot, for several reasons, be crafted effectively from within an education 'silo'.

Justice-enhancing education responses require an understanding of how pastoralist livelihoods work. I have here begun to identify 'terms of inclusion' associated with exogenously provided forms of education from a livelihoods-orientated perspective, and demonstrated their varying implications for livelihood sustainability. Making these terms visible moves us towards the kind of constructive appreciation of pastoralist rationales for seeking and resisting education inclusion that can inform a different kind of 'practical action' (Sen 2009) towards improving people's lives than is allowed by a negative framing of pastoralism.

Through this lens of investigation, 'education deprivation' is itself revealed as a potentially misleading descriptor, since it negates the prior existence of education among pastoralists, in the form of the situated learning on which their livelihood sustainability depends – although there is clearly a need to augment this with skills arising from exogenous education. When considering practical action, responses must take cognisance of pastoralists' potential vulnerability to livelihood insecurity, in contexts of extensive curtailing and privatisation of natural resources and restriction of the mobility on which pastoralism critically depends. This vulnerability has rather less to do with pastoralism itself than with the (mis)exercise of power by educated others, which further highlights disempowerment of education deprivation. It is incumbent on education provision to engage with the nuance and pluralism of these challenges.

The claim implicit in concern over 'education deprivation' that formal education is necessarily desirable must be treated with caution. 'Mainstream' formal education provision is cast within – and expected to reproduce – sedentary living as a largely unquestioned, hegemonic norm of human life. Analysis through a livelihoods lens reveals that the institutional arrangements of formal (day and boarding) schooling have been instrumental in marginalising pastoralists by imposing particularly demanding terms of inclusion – in relation not just to physical access, but also their orientation towards educating learners out of a mobile livelihood. This is done directly through curricular content, and indirectly by competing with opportunity to acquire situated livelihood knowledge. For those who seek an exit route from a pastoralist livelihood, this overarching term of inclusion may be acceptable – but failures of school quality and availability remain problematic. For those who do not, formal education's instrumentality in changing pastoralists into sedentary, educated, 'included' citizens may be resisted, pointing towards education deprivation as an injustice created by particular institutional arrangements.

Alternative basic education provision validates rather than undermines pastoralist livelihoods and is more inclined, and better able, than formal provision to tailor curricular content to respond to delivery contexts and offer terms of inclusion that favour girls' enrolment. Nevertheless, since social status deprivation (Kabeer 2006) is an integral facet of pastoralist marginalisation, including the 'hard to reach' through alternative provision that is livelihood sensitive, but lacks status equivalence, legitimises unequal institutional arrangements by implicitly supporting the mainstream/alternative dichotomy. Operationally, ODL has potential for positive practical action by offering terms of inclusion that embed formalised provision within a mobile pastoralist livelihood but, like 'mainstream' schooling, this model raises difficulties of curriculum relevance and what knowledge pastoralists seeking to remain within their mobile livelihood wish to acquire.

As the EFA and MDG target date approaches, there are welcome signs of global attention to the unsustainable use of resources, a challenge laid out in this UN-members' think piece: 'Today's world risks exceeding the limits of the earth's capacity in several critical dimensions' (UNSTT 2012, 3) and as, 'the natural resource base is destroyed … A realistic development agenda can no longer neglect the link among the economic, social and environmental dimensions of development' (3–4). Unlike much of humankind, pastoralists tread lightly on the planet. Once the myths about mobile pastoralism have been revealed as just that – faulty science and/or prejudiced interpretations – it becomes clear these millions of people – who already know how to live sustainably and have forms of education that pass this knowledge on to the next generation – are at the sharp edge of what is, if one were to put it strongly, the vandalism of 'educated' others. Action to address their 'education deprivation' would do well, under these circumstances, to focus on the positive contributions to the future of humankind that pastoralists make through their mobile livelihoods, to discard the 'hard to reach' label and to consider afresh where social injustice lies.

Notes

1. The word nomad came into English in the sixteenth century from French, via Latin from the Greek word *nomas* – wandering shepherd – related to *nemein*: to feed, pasture. Contemporary English usage (cf. Oxford English Dictionary) offers two ideas of a nomad: (1) as a member of a people or tribe who move from place to place to find pasture and food; and (2) a person who continually moves from place to place; a wanderer.
2. Further detail available at: http://www.huntercourse.com/blog/2011/05/amazing-hunter-gatherer-societies-still-in-existence/.
3. The term 'mobile pastoralist' highlights my focus on pastoralists who move. There are also sedentary pastoralists, and people who self-describe as pastoralists although they (now) pursue an alternative livelihood, referred to as 'exited' pastoralists.
4. Such provision demonstrates that quality assurance associated with learner retention demands real effort: USAID (2008, 25) gives an example from Ethiopia of an education supervisor responsible for monitoring, for the Afar Pastoralist Development Association, 14 classes across sites 120 km apart. Of those, 11 are only accessible by foot and their whereabouts are established by using local informants and tracking which, when the supervisor reaches it, is just as likely to deliver a vacated site as one where a school is currently running.
5. http://www.australiangeographic.com.au/journal/australias-school-of-the-air.htm.
6. Implementation is pending. Ministerial effort since 2010 has focused on setting up a 'competent and professional' Nomadic Commission that, with the added impetus arising from the Bill of Rights in the 2010 Constitution, is able to craft a 'coherent strategy' for all nomadic communities. Two legislative instruments supporting these purposes passed into law at the end of 2012 and impetus is again growing (personal communication, MDNKOAL representative, September 20, 2012).

References

African Union Commission. 2010. *Policy Framework for Pastoralism in Africa: Securing, Protecting and Improving the Lives, Livelihoods and Rights of Pastoralist Communities*. African Union Commission: Department of Rural Economy and Agriculture. Accessed October 19, 2012. http://au.int/en/dp/rea/sites/default/files/Policy%20Framework%20for%20Pastoralism.pdf

Agrawal, A., and V. Saberwal. 2004. "Whither South Asian Pastoralism? An Introduction." *Nomadic Peoples* 8 (2): 36–53. doi:10.3167/082279404780446113.

Akyeampong, K., K. Lussier, J. Pryor, and J. Westbrook. 2013. "Improving Teaching and Learning of Basic Maths and Reading in Africa: Does Teacher Prepara-
tion Count?" *International Journal of Educational Development* 33 (3): 272–
282. doi:10.1016/j.ijedudev.2012.09.006.

Andreasson, S. 2006. "Stand and Deliver: Private Property and the Politics of Global
Dispossession." *Political Studies* 54 (1): 3–22. doi:10.1111/post.2006.54.issue-1.

Arjona, C., A. Jamal, C. Menkel-Meadown, V. Ramjarj, and F. Satiro. 2012. "Sense
of Sen: Reflecting on Amartya Sen's Ideas of Justice." *International Journal of
Law* 8 (1): 155–178.

Bangsbo, E. 2008. "Schooling for Knowledge and Cultural Survival. Tibetan Community Schools in Nomadic Herding Areas." *Educational Review* 60 (1): 69–
84. doi:10.1080/00131910701794598.

Berry, N. 2010. "Bringing Books to Pastoralist Communities: Camel Libraries in the
Somali Region." In *Disaster Risk Reduction in the Drylands of the Horn of Africa*.
Newsletter of the Regional Learning & Advocacy Programme (REGLAP) for Vulnerable Dryland Communities. Accessed November 4, 2012. http://www.google.
co.uk/#hl=en&sclient=psy-*ab*&q=Save+the+Children+UK+Somalia+Camel+Library+
Berry+2010)+&oq=Save+the+Children+UK+Somalia+Camel+Library+Berry+2010)+
&gs_l=serp.3...35742.40621.3.41492.6.6.0.0.0.0.148.652.2j4.6.0.les%3B..0.0...1c.
1.IP43dAlpMoY&pbx=1&bav=on.2,or.r_gc.r_pw.r_qf.&fp=a0efe76d35983d56&
bpcl=37189454&biw=1520&bih=864

Blench, R. 2001. *'You Can't Go Home Again'. Pastoralism in the New Millennium*.
London: Overseas Development Institute.

Carr-Hill, R. 2006. "Educational Services and Nomadic Groups in Djibouti, Eritrea,
Ethiopia, Kenya, Tanzania and Uganda." In *The Education of Nomadic Peoples:
Current Issues, Future Prospects*, edited by C. Dyer, 35–52. Oxford: Berghahn.

Carr-Hill, R. 2012. "Finding and then Counting Out-of-School Children." *Compare*
42 (2): 187–212.

Chatty, D. 2006a. "Boarding Schools for Mobile People: The Harasiis in the Sul-
tanate of Oman." In *The Education of Nomadic Peoples: Current Issues, Future
Prospects*, edited by C. Dyer, 212–230. Oxford: Berghahn.

Chatty, D., ed. 2006b. *Nomadic Societies in the Middle East and North Africa:
Entering the 21st Century*, 431–462. Leiden: Brill.

Danaher, P., M. Kenny, and J. Leder, eds. 2009. *Traveller, Nomadic and Migrant
Education*. London: Routledge.

Demberel, and H. Penn. 2006. "Education and Pastoralism in Mongolia." In *The
Education of Nomadic Peoples: Current Issues, Future Prospects*, edited by C.
Dyer, 193–211. Oxford: Berghahn.

Devereux, S. 2010. "Better Marginalised than Incorporated? Pastoralist Livelihoods
in Somali Region, Ethiopia." *European Journal of Development Research* 22
(5): 678–695. doi:10.1057/ejdr.2010.29.

Dyer, C., ed. 2006. *The Education of Nomadic Peoples: Current Issues, Future
Prospects*. Oxford: Berghahn.

Dyer, C. 2008. "Literacies and Discourses of Development among the Rabaris of
Kutch, India." *Journal of Development Studies* 44 (6): 820–836.

Dyer, C. 2012. "Formal Education and Pastoralism in Western India: Inclusion, or
Adverse Incorporation?" *Compare* 42 (2): 259–282.

Dyer, C., ed. 2013. "Educating the Poorest." Special Issue of the *International
Journal of Educational Development*: 31 (3).

Dyer, C. 2014. *Nomads, Education and Development: Mobile Pastoralists and Education's Terms of Inclusion.* London: Routledge.

ECHO (European Commission Humanitarian Aid Department). 2009. *Get to Know Pastoralism – It Works! A Handbook for Journalists.* Nairobi, Kenya: Oxfam GB.

FAO. 2003. *The State of Food Insecurity in the World.* Rome: Food and Agriculture Organisation. http://www.fao.org/docrep/006/j0083e/j0083e.pdf

Galaty, J., and D. Johnston. 1990. "Introduction: Pastoral Systems in Global Perspective." In *The World of Pastoralism*, edited by J. Galaty and D. Johnston, 1–33. London: Belhaven.

Greany, K. 2012. "Education as Freedom? A Capability-Framed Exploration of Education Conversion among the Marginalised: The Case of Out-Migrant Karamojong Youth in Kampala." Unpublished PhD thesis, University of London.

Hickey, S., and A. du Toit. 2007. *Adverse Incorporation, Social Exclusion and Chronic Poverty.* Chronic Poverty Research Centre Working Paper 81. Accessed March 30, 2010. www.chronicpoverty.org/uploads/publication_files/WP81_Hickey_duToit.pdf

IGAD. 2007. *Report of the IGAD Regional Workshop on the Disarmament of Pastoralist Communities.* May 28–30, Entebbe, Uganda. The Inter-governmental Authority on Development. Accessed March 21, 2011. www.cewarn.org/index.php?option=com_docman&task=doc

IIED. 2009. *Modern and Mobile. The Future of Livestock Production in Africa's Drylands.* London: International Institute for Environment and Development, and SOS Sahel International UK.

Kabeer, N. 2006. "Social Exclusion and the MDGs: The Challenge of 'Durable Inequalities' in the Asian Context." Paper presented to the Asia 2010 Conference on Promoting Growth, Ending Poverty. Accessed March 30, 2011. http://www.eldis.org/vfile/upload/1/document/0708/DOC21178.pdf

Kenny, M., and P. Danaher. 2009. "Editorial Introduction: Three Dimensions of Changing Schools." In *Traveller, Nomadic and Migrant Education*, edited by P. Danaher, M. Kenny, and J. Remy Leder, 28–39. London: Routledge.

Klute, G. 1996. "Introduction." *Nomadic Peoples* 38: 3–10.

Krätli, S. 2001. *Education Provision to Nomadic Pastoralists: A Literature Review.* IDS Working Paper 126. New York: World Bank.

Krätli, S., and C. Dyer. 2009. *Mobile Pastoralists and Education: Strategic Options.* London: IIED. Accessed November 14, 2012. http://pubs.iied.org/pdfs/10021IIED.pdf

Lave, J., and E. Wenger. 1991. *Situated Learning: Legitimate Peripheral Participation.* Cambridge: Cambridge University Press. doi:10.1017/CBO9780511815355.

Lewin, K., and R. Sabates. 2011. *Changing Patterns of Access to Education in Anglophone and Francophone Countries in Sub Saharan Africa: Is Education for All Pro-Poor?* CREATE Pathway to Access Research Monograph No. 52. http://www.create-rpc.org/pdf_documents/PTA52.pdf

Little, P., J. McPeak, C. Barrett, and P. Kristjanson. 2008. *Challenging Orthodoxies: Understanding Poverty in Pastoral Areas of East Africa.* Accessed March 24, 2012. http://pdf.usaid.gov/pdf_docs/PNADM455.pdf

McCaffery, J., K. Sanni, C. Ezeomah, and J. Pennells. 2006. "Adult Literacy and Teacher Education in a Community Education Programme in Nigeria." In *The Education of Nomadic Peoples: Current Issues, Future Prospects*, edited by C. Dyer, 231–258. Oxford: Berghahn.

MDNKOAL. 2010. *Getting to the Hardest to Reach: A Strategy to Provide Education to Nomadic Communities in Kenya through Distance Learning.* Nairobi:

Minister of State for Development of Northern Kenya and Other Arid Lands (Office of the Prime Minister) and Education for Nomads Programme.

MoESTK. 2010. *Policy Guidelines on Nomadic Education in Kenya*. Republic of Kenya, Nairobi: The Ministry of Education.

MoESTK/UNICEF. 2006. *Forum on Flexible Education. Reaching Nomadic Populations, Garissa, Kenya, 20–23 June 2006. Summary Report*. Nairobi: Kenya Ministry of Education, UNICEF, Commonwealth of Learning.

Mortimore, M., S. Anderson, L. Cotula, J. Davies, K. Faccer, C. Hesse, J. Morton, W. Nyangena, J. Skinner, and C. Wolfangel. 2009. *Dryland Opportunities: A New Paradigm for People, Ecosystems and Development*. Gland (Switzerland), London and Nairobi: IUCN, IIED and UNDP/DDC.

Morton, J. 2010. "Why Should Governmentality Matter for the Study of Pastoral Development?" *Nomadic Peoples* 14 (1): 6–30. doi:10.3167/np.2010.140102.

Murphy, P., and F. Wolfenden. 2013. "Developing a Pedagogy of Mutuality in a Capability Approach: Teachers' Experiences of Using the Open Educational Resources (OER) of the Teacher Education in Sub-Saharan Africa (TESSA) Programme." *International Journal of Educational Development* 33 (3): 263–271. doi:10.1016/j.ijedudev.2012.09.010.

Nambi, V. Arivudai. 2001. "Modern Technology and New Forms of Nomadism: Duck Herders in Southern India." *Nomadic Peoples* 5 (1): 155–167. doi:10.3167/082279401782310943

Niamir-Fuller, M. 1999. Managing Mobility in African Rangelands." In *Managing Mobility in African Rangelands: The Legitimization of Transhumance*, edited by M. Niamr-Fuller, 102–131. London: Intermediate Technology Publications. Accessed October 19, 2012. http://www.ifpri.org/sites/default/files/pubs/pubs/books/proprights/proprights_ch04.pdf

Nori, M. 2007. *Mobile Livelihoods, Patchy Resources and Shifting Rights: Approaching Pastoral Territories: An Issues Paper*. Rome: International Land Coalition. Accessed November 4, 2012. http://www.hubrural.org/IMG/pdf/ilc_document_territoires_pastoraux_eng.pdf

Oxfam. 2009. *TEFA Strategic Plan 2009–2013*. Nairobi: Oxfam GB.

Pattison, J. 2011. "Orma Livelihoods in Tana River District, Kenya: A Study of Constraints, Adaptation and Innovation." Unpublished PhD diss, University of Edinburgh.

PEAS. nd. *Pastoralist Area Education Strategy*. Ethiopia. Accessed March 28, 2011. www.ethiopia.gov.et/.../Pastralest%20Education%20stratege%20Eng.pdf

Perraton, H. 2007. *Open and Distance Learning in the Developing World*. 2nd ed. Routledge Studies in Distance Education. London and New York: Routledge.

Rao, A. 2006. "The Acquisition of Manners, Morals and Knowledge: Growing into and out of Bakkarwal Society." In *The Education of Nomadic Peoples: Current Issues, Future Prospects*, edited by C. Dyer, 53–76. Oxford: Berghahn.

Rao, A., and M. Casimir. 2003. "Nomadism in South Asia: An Introduction." In *Nomadism in South Asia*, edited by A. Rao and M. Casimir, 1–38. New Delhi: Oxford University Press.

Ruto, S., Z. Ongweny, and J. Mugo. 2009. *Educational Marginalisation in Northern Kenya, Background Paper to the 'Education for All Global Monitoring Report 2010*. Nairobi.

Sanou, S., and S. Aikman. 2005. "Pastoralist Schools in Mali. Gendered Roles and Curriculum Realities." In *Beyond Access. Transforming Policy and Practice for Gender Inequality in Education*, edited by S. Aikman and E. Unterhalter, 181–195. Oxford: Oxfam GB.

Scoones, I., ed. 1995. *Living with Uncertainty: New Directions in Pastoral Development in Africa*. London: Intermediate Technology Publications.

Scoones, I. 2009. "Livelihoods Perspectives and Rural Development." *Journal of Peasant Studies* 36 (1): 171–196. doi:10.1080/03066150902820503.

Scott, J. 1998. *Seeing Like a State: How Certain Schemes to Improve the Human Condition Have Failed*. New York: Yale University Press.

Sen, A. 2009. *The Idea of Justice*. Cambridge, MA: Harvard University Press.

Shahbazi, M. 2006. "The Qashqa'i: Formal Education and the Indigenous Educators." In *The Education of Nomadic Peoples: Current Issues, Future Prospects*, edited by C. Dyer, 175–192. Oxford: Berghahn.

Sharma, V., I. Köhler-Rollefson, and J. Morton. 2003. "Pastoralism in India: A Scoping Study." http://www.dfid.gov.uk/r4d/PDF/outputs/ZC0181b.pdf

Steiner-Khamsi, G., and I. Stolpe. 2005. "Non-Traveling Best Practices for a Traveling Population: The Case of Nomadic Education in Mongolia." *European Educational Research Journal* 4 (1): 22–35. doi:10.2304/eerj.

Tahir, G. 1997. "Nomadic Education in Nigeria." In *The Education of Nomadic Populations in Africa*, Vol. I, edited by C. Ezeomah. Breda: UNESCO.

du Toit, A. 2005. *Forgotten by the Highway: Globalisation, Adverse Incorporation and Chronic Poverty in a Commercial Farming District*. CSSR Working Paper No. 101, Centre for Social Science Research, University of Cape Town. Accessed January 26, 2011. http://www. sarpn.org.za/documents/d0001207/P1339-CSSR_DuToit_Febr2005.pdf

UNDP. 2003. *Pastoralism and Mobility in the Drylands*. The Global Drylands Imperative (June 2003). http://www.iucn.org/wisp/whatwisp/why_a_global_initiative_on_pastoralism_/?2313/Misconceptions-surrounding-pastoralism

UNESCO. 2010. *Reaching the Marginalized*. EFA Global Monitoring Report. Accessed November 4, 2012. http://unesdoc.unesco.org/images/0018/001866/186606e.pdf

UNSTT. 2012. *Building on the MDGs to Bring Sustainable Development to the Post-2015 Development Agenda*. Thematic Think Piece. UN System Task Team on the post 2015 UN Development Agenda. Accessed November 2, 2012. http://www.un.org/millenniumgoals/pdf/Think%20Pieces/17_sustainable_development.pdf

USAID. 2008. "Education for Pastoralists: Flexible Approaches." http://pdf.usaid.gov/pdf_docs/PNADN691.pdf

USAID. 2012. "Mobile Schools: Serving Nomadic Pastoralist Communities in North Eastern Province." Accessed November 4, 2012. http://kenya.usaid.gov/programs/education-and-youth/1015

WDEFA. 1990. "World Declaration of Education for All: Meeting Basic Learning Needs." World Conference on Education for All, Jomtien, Thailand.

de Weijer, F. 2005. *Towards a Pastoralist Support Strategy*. USAID/RAMP. Accessed November 4, 2012. http://community.eldis.org/?233@@.5994401e!enclosure=.5994401f

Woldemichael, B. 1995. *Education for the Pastoral Communities of Eritrea: A Research Study*. Asmara: Ministry of Education and Swedish Save the Children.

Combining identity and integration: comparative analysis of schools for two minority groups in Ukraine

Volodymyr Kulyk

Institute of Political and Ethnic Studies, National Academy of Sciences of Ukraine, Kyiv, Ukraine

This article analyses school systems for two of Ukraine's minorities, the Hungarians and the Crimean Tatars with the aim of assessing their success in promoting ethnocultural identity and social integration of the minority youth. I demonstrate that the exclusive instruction in Hungarian ensures the reproduction of group language knowledge and identity among the minority members but perpetuates their inability to communicate in the majority language and thus limits their social mobility. In contrast, the limited scope of education in Crimean Tatar exacerbates the problem of its poor knowledge by the group members and, therefore, vulnerability of their cultural identity. I argue that the introduction of bilingual education is the best way to solve the two groups' educational problems.

Introduction

Language processes in the educational domain of Ukrainian and other post-Soviet societies have usually been studied in terms of interplay between the greater role of the titular language, on the one hand, and linguistic rights of the Russian-speakers, on the other (Janmaat 2000; Bilaniuk and Melnyk 2008; Pavlenko 2011). The prominence of the 'Russian question' in education and other domains where linguistic rights are implemented results both from sheer numbers of ethnic Russians and other Russian-speakers and from the defense of their rights by the Russian kin-state and, in some countries, by influential domestic parties. The controversy over the alleged discrimination against Russian-speakers has diverted public and scholarly attention from problems of other minorities, which in some cases are much more severe. Moreover, it has thus been overseen that the educational situation differs considerably from one of these smaller groups to another (but see Stewart 2005).

In another omission, the language regime of education has mostly been examined from the point of view of nation building and minority rights

56

rather than that of students' learning progress and future life chances (e.g. Janmaat 2000; Pavlenko 2011). An underlying assumption seems to have been that members of all ethnic groups would prefer – and benefit from – education in their eponymous languages if it were not for the state's nationalising intervention. However, this assumption is more reflective of many scholars' essentialist emphasis on the role of ethnic identity in people's behaviour than it is of parents' preferences, which may be primarily shaped by considerations of educational efficiency or post-education utility. Rather than relating education first and foremost to politics, with its conflicts over perceived group interests, scholarly analyses should also view it as part of social and economic processes that determine the performance of educational establishments, the value of skills that students acquire in the process of education and, therefore, their preferences regarding this process.

This article seeks to confront the above-mentioned shortcomings. It analyses in detail the situations of two groups, the Hungarians of Transcarpathia and the Crimean Tatars of the Crimean peninsula, whose educational conditions (as well as social and cultural conditions in general) differed sharply during the Soviet time and remain very different after two decades of independence. I try to demonstrate how both the preservation of inherited facilities with the exclusive instruction in Hungarian and the limited introduction of education in Crimean Tatar have created serious problems for social integration and/or ethnocultural identity of the cohorts under consideration.

Minority education between identity and integration

Education is a crucial agent of socialisation, which is 'concerned with the insertion of "newcomers" into existing cultural and socio-political settings' (Biesta 2007, 27) or, more specifically, with preparing them 'to fit successfully into the internal environment of the community of their upbringing and into the external environment' of a wider society (Thomas and Wahrhaftig 1971, 231). This double orientation manifests itself in the choice of organisation of the educational process, knowledge and skills to be taught and the language(s) to be used. Since the introduction of state-provided mass education, the authorities in would-be national states have sought to unify the structure and content of education and orient it toward the perceived needs of entire society rather than of particular groups, even though this perception has primarily been patterned at the upper class. This was reflected, in particular, in a strong emphasis on the formation of loyal citizens of the state and the promotion of their identification with the eponymous nation (Meyer 1977). National identification and social cohesion were also promoted by the use of the titular language as the medium of instruction and extracurricular activities. Such nationalising drive precluded valorisation of particular historical memories, cultural artifacts and language varieties of (subordinate) social or ethnolinguistic groups.

In contrast, multinational empires, while promoting the knowledge and use of the metropolitan language among the elites, allowed or even encouraged mass education in local languages and with some local content. In the nineteenth century, the most advanced system of multilingual education was established in the Austro-Hungarian Empire incorporating western Ukrainian regions. In the twentieth century, a far more radical multinational project was carried out in the USSR, which came to include almost all Ukrainian-populated territories. In Ukraine, as in other 'national' republics, the titular language was used alongside Russian in education and other public practices, although the former language increasingly gave way to the latter (Martin 2001; Burger 2003).

In the last decades, the democratisation of the public domain in many states across the globe allowed group elites to pressure for a balance between the educational goals of socialisation into the society and into the community or, put another way, social integration and the preservation of particular identities. As far as the language regime is concerned, many ethnic-based varieties have been recognised as languages and introduced, to a varying degree, into the educational process. In the most pluralist case, some of the so-called autochthonous minorities in Western societies were allowed to create a system of monolingual education in their group languages. While the established European nation-states are more tolerant of minority education than they were in the past, considerations of loyalty and integration of minority members have led some post-communist states to curtail the monolingual education in the languages of formerly dominant groups (Hogan-Brun 2006). At the same time, immigrant languages in the USA and Western Europe can at best be used in transitional bilingual education intended to ensure that students do not fall behind while they are learning the majority language (Cummins 1989). Similarly, in most African countries the instruction in local languages is limited to primary education, while secondary schools teach in the former colonial languages, which continue to dominate the public sphere (Bamgbose 2004).

The language regimes of minority education have been studied from several main perspectives, reflecting scholars' disciplinary and ideological preferences and dominant patterns in their respective countries. Language-policy scholars analysed the use of minority languages in education as a result of political struggle between majority and minority elites as well as between national governments and international organisations. A related body of minority-rights studies measured educational conditions of minority youth by the yardstick of their assumed willingness to be instructed in their group languages. It is these two approaches that have been taken in most studies of minority education in Ukraine and other countries of the former USSR, which examine it in the context of state efforts to promote the titular language as a factor of post-imperial nation-building (Janmaat 2000; Stewart 2005; Ciscel 2008; Kalynovs'ka 2009).

Quite different perspectives have dominated analyses of the educational contexts of Western countries, in particular the USA, where the use of minority languages even as a transitional stage came under attack in view of its allegedly negative impact on the acquisition of the dominant language. Pedagogical and psychological studies sought to explain the relatively low educational performance of minority students and variation across minority groups. The authors argued that scholars should go beyond the educational domain and 'look not only at the social structure of the host society and the cultural background of the minority group, but also at the minority groups' situation in the host society, including its perceptions of the opportunities available and the historical context of its relationship to the dominant group' (Gibson 1993, 123–4). For their part, anthropological studies examined the discursive dynamics of the educational process in order to reveal underlying ideologies of language and education and demonstrate how these reflect the interests of certain groups who 'are in a position to assign value to … cultural and linguistic capital' (Martin-Jones and Heller 1996, 129).

In Ukraine, pedagogical studies of minority education have been rather few and not always based on an empirical analysis of student performance or parental choice (among exceptions, see Chernyi 2005; Szilágyi 2009). Anthropological and sociological studies of Ukrainian education usually dealt with the language dimension only on the margin and those few that focused on this dimension were set in contexts with no 'truly' minority languages – that is, other than Russian (e.g. Søvik 2007; Polese 2010). Students of minority education in Ukraine thus do not make use of many methods that have proved effective in analyses of educational processes elsewhere.

Design of the study

With these shortcomings in mind, I combine various approaches in order to examine the function of two sets of minority-language educational establishments in Ukraine. While grounded in language policy, my study also pays attention to the economic situation of the Hungarian and Crimean Tatar educational systems, students' school performance and their perceptions of available opportunities in adulthood. On the one hand, I seek to assess the two systems' success in promoting ethnocultural identity and social integration of the minority youth. On the other, I want to examine beliefs of students and parents regarding the appropriate language regime of minority education and compare them with ideologies espoused by minority elites and largely embodied in the school systems themselves.

The main methods employed in the study are semi-structured interviews with educational officials and minority activists and questionnaires administered to graduating students and their parents. Both kinds of data were collected during a week-long trip to the relevant regions in February and May 2008, respectively. In each case, I studied five schools in different parts of the province. In Transcarpathia, I chose three localities with Hungarian majority (the town of Berehove and villages of Dertsen, Mukacheve district, and Ianoshi, Berehove district) and two with Hungarian minority (provincial center of Uzhhorod and city of Mukacheve). In Crimea, where the Crimean Tatars do not constitute a majority in any sizable locality, I chose the provincial center of Simferopol, the towns of Bakhchysarai, Sudak and Zuia and the village of Kolchuhyne, Simferopol district.

My interviewees included the directors of the examined schools, heads of the educational departments of the respective state administrations and leaders of influential organisations of the minorities (see Appendix). The questionnaire was administered among all present students of the graduating classes (grade 11). The total number of respondents constituted 125 in Transcarpathia and 130 in Crimea, although some students failed to respond to certain questions. A complementary parental questionnaire was administered in two schools of each region (Berehove and Dertsen in Transcarpathia and Bakhchysarai and Simferopol in Crimea), where the school authorities distributed it among those high-school students (grades 11 and 10) whose parents they expected to respond. Their answers are thus far from representative for all parents of these schools, so I will only use them to indicate clear preferences and predominant motivations.

Minority education in Ukraine

Prior to analysing educational situations of the two selected groups, it is appropriate to characterise Ukraine's minority education in general. The most prominent process in post-Soviet Ukrainian education has been a dramatic decrease in the number of schools and other establishments with instruction in Russian. During the Soviet times, Russian was the main language of higher education and prestigious employment, both in Ukraine and beyond, which urged many Ukrainians and members of other minorities to have their children educated in Russian, thus paving the way for their assimilation. After the proclamation of Ukraine's independence, education became the first domain to experience a large-scale 'de-Russification', which was intended to undo the Soviet policies and contribute to the 'building' of a post-imperial Ukrainian nation with the titular language as one if its unifying elements. Although in the heavily Russified eastern and southern regions the transition was very slow, Ukrainian has ultimately become the dominant language of instruction everywhere except for Crimea and the Donbas. But then this Ukrainianization remains rather formal, as in most urban schools students usually switch to Russian during breaks and those from Ukrainian-speaking families arguably feel the pressure to adjust to the dominant pattern (Stepanenko 1999, 95–141; Janmaat 2000, 67–120; Bilaniuk and Melnyk 2008, 351–61; Kalynovs'ka 2009, 205–15).

Apart from the 'de-Russifying' efforts, the state's attitude towards instruction in minority languages has been rather favourable. The Soviet idea of the appropriateness of educating children in their native/group language was retained and, as far as non-Russian minorities were concerned, implemented more fully than in the Soviet period. In addition to the inherited system of state-supported schools with Russian, Romanian/Moldovan, Hungarian and Polish languages of instruction, there appeared schools or separate classes (streams) teaching in Crimean Tatar, Slovak and Bulgarian. The state provided funding for minority schools, published textbooks and trained teachers in special departments of universities. Moreover, it usually did not impede attempts of the kin-states to help solve remaining problems of the respective groups' schools, such as a lack of furniture, equipment or books in the group language (Chilachava and Pylypenko 2004, 166–76; Stewart 2005, 112, 125).

The schooling in minority languages was affected by general flaws of the educational system as well as by additional problems of minority education and specific conditions of each group. In general, the protracted economic crisis and a low priority of education on the government's agenda caused extremely low salaries for teachers, resulting in a loss of skilled personnel, a lack of textbooks and inadequate maintenance of buildings. For minority schools, these problems were supplemented by cost and time for translating textbooks into their respective languages of instruction, since they were required to use the same books as Ukrainian-language schools, except for minority-specific subjects. An even more serious problem was teaching of the Ukrainian language and literature, for which there were few qualified teachers because in the Soviet time these schools had taught Russian as the second language and offered no Ukrainian lessons at all (Chilachava and Pylypenko 2004, 169–72; interview Hertsoh). Moreover, the approach to teaching Ukrainian failed to take into account the fact that it was a second language for minority students, many of who had little contact with it beyond the classroom (Chernychko 2009, 98–101; interviews Lendiel, Mitsyk). This resulted in poor knowledge of Ukrainian among graduates of minority-language schools, which led most of them (except for those educated in the widely-used Russian) to stay in places of their group's prevalence or leave for higher education and/or employment in kin-states.

Minority leaders tried to resist this unfortunate tendency by demanding that their languages be used, alongside Ukrainian, in institutions of higher education in regions of the respective groups' concentration or at least in examinations for admission thereto. At the same time, both the realisation of the inadequacy of the exclusively minority-language system for social integration and the wish to use the instruction in the titular language as an instrument of nation-building led the Ministry of Education to introduce some elements of Ukrainian (Stewart 2005, 114–29). A resolute change came in early-2008 when newly appointed minister Ivan Vakarchuk introduced independent external evaluation (or testing, as it became popularly known) of all school graduates, which was to be mandatory for admission to any institutions of higher education. This move was primarily meant to combat rampant corruption in schools and universities by disconnecting the evaluation of graduating students from decision-making on their future (Bazhal 2008). However, the minister used this change as an excuse for the long-planned transition to entrance examinations (now replaced by tests) in the state language only. This move was part of the state effort to increase the use of Ukrainian in various domains, which became more pronounced under then President Viktor Yushchenko (Kulyk 2009, 24–35).

Minority educators and activists resolutely objected to this plan, which would arguably put the minority youth at a disadvantage. The protests made Vakarchuk allow a transitory period of two years, during which the minority-language students had to work on their Ukrainian. For this purpose, a ministerial decree envisaged gradual introduction of the state language for teaching of various subjects (U shkolakh 2008). However, the minister did not agree to postpone a mandatory test in the Ukrainian language and literature. Moreover, the two-year period was widely viewed by educators as too short for making minority students ready to take all tests in Ukrainian as of 2010. But then, on the eve of the announced transition, Vakarchuk left his office in the wake of Yushchenko's failure in the 2010 election. The new minister Dmytro Tabachnyk decided for the continued use of six minority languages in external evaluation and as exclusive mediums in the respective schools (Riabchun 2010).

The above description of the minority education in general should not imply the uniformity across the regions and ethnic groups. Although most of the above-described problems have indeed been common to all minorities, their severity and relative priority depend on specific conditions of a particular group in a particular region. On the one hand, a persistent lack of funding means that those minorities that inherited educational facilities in their group language had a strong advantage over those for who such facilities had to be created anew. On the other, the relationship between the majority and a minority and between Ukraine and the respective kin-state influenced the readiness of the authorities to allot available resources for that minority's needs. Perhaps no two groups demonstrate these effects better than the Hungarians and the Crimean Tatars.

The situation of Transcarpathian Hungarians

The Hungarians compactly residing in the south-western region of Transcarpathia (Zakarpattia) can serve as an illustration of the accommodating approach of the Ukrainian state toward the minorities' educational needs. The region where the Hungarians had been living since the ninth century was part of Hungarian-dominated entities until World War I, after which in was awarded to the newly established Czechoslovak state, seized again by Hungary with Hitler's dismemberment of that state in 1939 and annexed by the USSR in 1945. By making it part of the Ukrainian republic, the Soviet leadership inadvertently paved the way for its current position as a province of independent Ukraine. According to the 2001 census, there were about 151,500 Hungarians in Transcarpathia, where they constituted 12.1% of the population and were largely concentrated along the border with Hungary (All-Ukrainian Population Census n.d).

Apart from compact settlement, their knowledge of the group language was facilitated by general access to broadcasting from Hungary and a system of pre-school and school education in Hungarian. This system was originally created in Austria-Hungary, then drastically reduced during the Czechoslovak rule, shut down by the Soviets for the first decade of their control and, finally, reinstated in the 1950s (Vardy 1989, 68–74). The independent Ukrainian state has not only retained but also expanded the system. In the school year 2007/2008, when I conducted my field research, there were 71 schools with the instruction in Hungarian and 27 bilingual schools having Hungarian-language classes. The total number of students taught in that language constituted 17,366, or 10.5% of all school students of the region, which is close to the group's share in the general population (Zadovolennia n/d).

That these conditions enable the reproduction of the group's competence in Hungarian and reliance on it as the main everyday language is vividly demonstrated by the results of my questionnaire, administered to graduating students of Hungarian-language schools. As Table 1 shows, most of the students reported that they used primarily Hungarian in communication with parents and friends, watching television and reading books and periodicals. The reliance on Hungarian turned out to be particularly overwhelming in places of the group's prevalence. In those localities where Hungarians constitute a clear minority, the students used Ukrainian and Russian much more extensively but far from predominantly.

The treatment of these schools on the part of the authorities has been quite favourable. All of my interviewees denied any facts of discrimination in the allocation of funds, textbooks or any supplies. Moreover, much help came from the Hungarian authorities and private foundations. Not only did these sources facilitate renovation or construction of school buildings, replacement of furniture and stocking of libraries, but also every family with children instructed in Hungarian received an allowance from a foundation in Hungary (interview Mitsyk). Hungarian funding also made possible the functioning of a private Hungarian-language institution of higher education in Berehove, whose graduates helped reduce the deficit of schools teachers. At the same time, many teachers and other specialists were educated at several state-funded colleges in Transcarpathia, having parallel groups with the instruction in Hungarian (interview Hertsoh).

In the 1990s and early-2000s, many graduates of Transcarpathian Hungarian-language schools went to study and/or work in Hungary which,

Table 1. Self-reported language use of graduating students of five Hungarian-language schools in communicating with parents and friends, watching television, and reading books, newspapers and magazines, for the sample as a whole and separately for Hungarian-majority and Hungarian-minority localities (in percentage).

	Communication with parents (n = 125)			Communication with friends (n = 122)			Watching television (n = 121)			Reading books, periodicals (n = 119)		
	All	Hungarian majority	Hungarian minority	All	Hungarian majority	Hungarian minority	All	Hungarian majority	Hungarian minority	All	Hungarian majority	Hungarian minority
Mostly Hungarian	73.6	87.2	51.1	58.2	77.3	27.7	52.1	72.0	19.6	53.8	70.3	26.7
Mostly Ukrainian	3.2	0.0	8.5	9.8	1.3	23.4	3.3	0.0	8.7	5.9	0.0	15.6
Equally Hungarian and Ukrainian	17.6	11.5	27.7	29.5	21.3	42.6	19.8	14.7	28.3	28.0	28.4	31.1
Other	5.6	1.3	12.8	2.5	0.0	6.4	24.8	13.3	43.5	12.2	1.4	26.7

Note: For communication with parents, the third option means speaking Hungarian with one parent and Ukrainian with the other. The fourth option mostly pertains to the use of Russian mainly or on a par with Hungarian and Ukrainian.

in turn, contributed to the popularity of these schools (interview Arpa). However, the gradual improvement of economic situation in Ukraine, together with the toughening of the conditions for students and workers from abroad in Hungary, caused the reorientation of Transcarpathian graduates to work and study in their own region. The responses to the questionnaires support the statements of both Hungarian and Ukrainian interviewees. Only one-in-six students said they intended to study or work in Hungary. In contrast, four-out-of-five declared their wish for studying in Transcarpathia, most of these in the Ukrainian language. Most of parent respondents also preferred their children' studying and working in the region.

However, this preference was not matched by the graduates' adequate knowledge of Ukrainian, even among those intending to use it in higher education. Less than a third of respondents said they could speak Ukrainian 'very well' or 'well', while the same share evaluated their level as poor (see Table 2). Scores for the writing ability turned out somewhat higher, which reveals the primary orientation of the Ukrainian language education towards writing or, one may say, the most perceptible deficit in oral skills. Still, less than a half of respondents considered their knowledge to be very good or good. Naturally, in places of Hungarian prevalence the level of spoken Ukrainian was particularly low. Perhaps the most striking evidence of inadequate knowledge of the state language is the fact that in Berehove, three students refused to answer my Ukrainian-language questionnaire and simply wrote on their sheets 'Don't understand', while further two failed to answer the second, more complicated half of the questionnaire.

Given such poor knowledge of Ukrainian, it is not surprising that 58% of respondents would like to have external evaluation in Hungarian only, with further 31% opting for Hungarian 'in most subjects' (which might mean all subjects but the Ukrainian language and literature). Even among those who planned to study in Ukrainian, four-out-of-five preferred to pass

Table 2.   Self-reported levels of oral and written Ukrainian-language skills of graduating students of five Hungarian-language schools for the sample as a whole and separately for Hungarian-majority and Hungarian-minority localities (in percentage).

	Speaking in Ukrainian ($n = 119$)			Writing in Ukrainian ($n = 121$)		
	All	Hungarian majority	Hungarian minority	All	Hungarian majority	Hungarian minority
Very good	6.7	2.8	12.8	5.0	2.7	8.5
Good	23.5	15.3	36.2	37.2	37.8	36.2
Mediocre	39.5	38.9	40.4	47.1	50.0	42.6
Poor	30.3	43.1	10.6	10.7	9.5	12.8

evaluations exclusively or mainly in Hungarian, meaning that they did not rely on their current knowledge of Ukrainian and intended to improve it in the process of university studies. A few months later, the results of the tests confirmed their poor knowledge of Ukrainian. The students of the Hungarian-language schools I had studied scored much worse in the Ukrainian language and literature than in all other subjects for which they were free to use Hungarian, and much worse than students of those Ukrainian-language schools with whom they were equal in other subjects.[1] Thus, the policy intended to ensure school graduates' knowledge of the state language put the Hungarian youth at a disadvantage in competition for free admission to institutions of higher education and, accordingly, hindered their career chances.

Some interviewees viewed the continued use of Hungarian for admission to universities as the only way to ensure its speakers' right to higher education. They argued that graduates of minority-language schools would never know Ukrainian as well as those who had been instructed therein, hence, evaluation solely in the state language would always mean discrimination (e.g. interviews Hertsoh, Kovach). In effect, they called for the reversion to the situation that had existed before the introduction of external evaluation with the Ukrainian language as a mandatory subject (if not yet the only medium), even if that meant poor knowledge of the state language and, therefore, restricted mobility. One minority activist explicitly presented this choice as a preference of what is good 'for the nation' over what is 'not bad for parents and the child' (interview Medvid'), thus articulating the nationalist ideology prioritising national interests over individual ones.

At the same time, many students, parents and teachers did not share this priority. They believed that status quo (ante) could not be considered adequate for the long term and, therefore, supported the view that some changes should be made in order to ensure better knowledge of Ukrainian among Hungarian youth. In all, 62% of student respondents firmly or hesitantly agreed that it was worth teaching some subjects in their school in Ukrainian 'to make graduates' further study and work easier'. Most parents also shared this view, as did many of the directors and higher-level officials (e.g. interviews Arpa, Bubniak). Actually, some directors told me that they were already introducing elements of Ukrainian, which most students and parents supported. Moreover, many parents allegedly requested that the number of lessons of the Ukrainian language be increased (interviews Arpa, Mitsyk, Oros).

Still, some believed that such transformation of the minority education might evoke protests or at least complaints. Therefore, they wanted the state to retain the schools with exclusive instruction in Hungarian and let those parents willing to ensure their children's command of Ukrainian send them to majority schools (interviews Hertsoh, Mitsyk). Actually, most interviewees argued that this process was already under way (e.g. interviews

Bubniak, Lendiel). They believed that it might soon lead to drastic changes in the educational situation, while differing in their assessments thereof as either a laudable contribution to social integration or a regrettable path to a loss of group identity (e.g. interviews Oros, Kovach). But then the later revocation of the planned transition to tests exclusively in Ukrainian may have made these people more optimistic and less willing to accept any changes.

The situation of Crimean Tatars

The case of the Crimean Tatars provides a vivid illustration of the inability of the Ukrainian state to ensure equally favourable treatment of all ethnocultural groups. Although most problems specific to this group were inherited from the USSR, the Ukrainian authorities failed to effectively solve them due to a lack of resources, experience and, in many cases, goodwill, all the more so because the support for one group often ran counter to the perceived interests of another.

The Crimean Tatars are predominantly concentrated in the Crimean peninsula in the south of Ukraine and constitute the same share of the population of the region as the Hungarians in Transcarpathia (12%), despite being larger in numerical terms, namely 243,400 people in 2001 (All-Ukrainian Population Census n.d). The equality of relative sizes highlights the groups' unequal opportunities to use their languages in education, although they have partly to do with more dispersed settlement of the Crimean Tatars. In the school year of 2007–2008, the Crimean Tatars had only 15 schools with the instruction in their group language as well as separate classes in 62 bi- or tri-lingual schools. The total number of schoolchildren taught in Crimean Tatar was thrice as low as those instructed in Hungarian (5903 versus 17,366), which meant almost five times as low a share of group members. Only 16.6% of the Crimean Tatars schoolchildren were taught in the group language, while others attended schools with the instruction in the language of the peninsula's majority, Russian or, in some cases, in the state language of Ukraine. About 17% of Crimean Tatar students did not learn the group language even as a subject (Izuchenie n/d).

This inequality is rooted in the discrimination against the Crimean Tatars under the Soviet rule, which influenced their position in post-Soviet Ukraine, the majority's attitudes toward them and their own views and resources determining the applicability of different models of education. After centuries of independent statehood, the Crimean Tatars became subjects of Russian tsars in 1783 and underwent discriminatory treatment, which led to a large-scale emigration. When the Russian Empire was transformed into the multinational Soviet state, they found themselves in a national territorial autonomy with educational and cultural facilities in their group language. This cultural renaissance came to an abrupt end in 1944, with the wholesale deportation of the group (accused of having voluntary collaborated with the Nazi occupiers) from Crimea to Asian parts of the former USSR. For several decades, the Crimean Tatars were deprived of education in the eponymous language and largely lost fluency in it, particularly the youth.[2] Upon return to Crimea in the late-1980s and early-1990s, the deportees and their descendants were met with a lack of housing, land, jobs, schools and other social services as well as with the hostile or indifferent attitudes of most officials and residents guided by old Soviet stereotypes and new fears of interethnic confrontation. Although the central government was rather supportive of the needs of the returnees, it lacked resources for meeting them and was apprehensive about provoking discontent of the peninsula's Russian majority (Allworth 1998; European Commission against Racism and Intolerance 2011, 27–8).

Crimean Tatar leaders viewed education in the ancestral language as a crucial factor of the preservation of the people's language and identity (Concept 2007; interviews Chubarov, Kadzhametova). However, unlike other ethnic groups, Crimean Tatars' demands for education in their group language were in the beginning met only under strong pressure, often escalating into violent action. In view of the of the authorities' reluctance to provide buildings for their schools, parents and activists repeatedly resorted to seizures of aspired state property, while official decisions on the establishment of schools or classes often resulted from rallies and petitions. Still, most schools had to work in converted buildings which lacked necessary facilities and sometimes were in a very poor condition. Moreover, many villages and towns with a considerable share of Crimean Tatars had no instruction in the group's language, or it was limited to classes on the primary level (interviews Kadzhametova, Seitvelieva). The non-Tatar educational officials denied any prejudice of the authorities against the group but admitted that newly established schools for the returnees had to work under worse conditions than mainstream facilities built and equipped in the Soviet times (interview Pekhar).

Crimean Tatar cultural elites tend to believe that only separate schools with the instruction in the group's language and cultivation of its culture can create an environment contributing to the preservation of ethnocultural identity (Concept 2007; interview Kadzhametova). A crucial component of this mission (unfamiliar to those minorities mostly using their group languages in everyday life) is to ensure a good command of the Crimean Tatar language, which many students can not get at home or maintain in other practices. Students of the Crimean Tatar-language schools seem to come from rather exceptional families who consider knowledge of 'native language' and 'national culture' a high priority (cf. Chernyi 2005). Most parent respondents indicated these motives for having enrolled their children in minority-language schools. Despite this background, not all students speak the group language with parents and few use it in communication with friends, watching TV or reading books and periodicals, as demonstrated by

Table 3. Self-reported language use of graduating students of five Crimean Tatar-language schools in communicating with parents and friends, watching television and reading books, newspapers and magazines for the sample as a whole and separately for the city of Simferopol (in percentage).

	Communication with parents		Communication with friends		Watching television		Reading books, periodicals	
	All (n = 130)	Simferopol (n = 39)	All (n = 130)	Simferopol (n = 39)	All (n = 129)	Simferopol (n = 39)	All (n = 129)	Simferopol (n = 38)
Mostly in Crimean Tatar	60.8	12.8	11.5	0.0	2.3	0.0	14.7	2.6
Mostly in Russian	18.5	43.6	39.2	76.9	3.9	7.7	25.6	52.6
Equally in Crimean Tatar and Russian	20.0	41.0	47.7	17.9	9.3	7.7	31.8	10.5
Other	0.8	2.6	1.2	5.1	84.5	84.5	27.9	34.2

Note: For communication with parents, the third option means speaking Crimean Tatar with one parent and Russian with the other. The fourth option primarily pertains to the use of Ukrainian along with Crimean Tatar and/or Russian.

Table 4. Self-reported levels of the speaking and writing skills in Crimean Tatar, Ukrainian and Russian by graduating students of five Crimean Tatar-language schools (in percentage) for the sample as a whole ($n = 130$) and separately for the city of Simferopol ($n = 39$).

| | Crimean Tatar | | | | Ukrainian | | | | Russian | | | |
| | Speaking | | Writing | | Speaking | | Writing | | Speaking | | Writing | |
	All	Simferopol	All	Simferopol	All	Simferopol	All	Simferopol	All	Simferopol	All	Simferopol
Very good	24.6	7.7	22.3	5.1	16.9	28.2	16.9	35.9	49.6	59.0	26.9	41.0
Good	47.7	41.0	56.2	56.4	59.2	48.7	55.4	38.5	44.2	41.0	63.8	51.3
Mediocre	20.0	30.8	16.2	25.6	20.0	20.5	22.3	23.1	3.9	0.0	6.9	7.7
Poor	7.7	20.5	5.4	12.8	3.8	2.6	5.4	2.6	2.3	0.0	2.3	0.0

the responses of graduating students of five schools (see Table 3). The reliance on the majority language turned out to be particularly heavy in the city of Simferopol. Everywhere the primary language of speaking with friends and reading was Russian, while Ukrainian was widely used, alongside the other two languages, only for watching television.[3]

Given such limited use of both Crimean Tatar and Ukrainian outside of school, it is remarkable how well the students believed they knew those languages. Only about a quarter of respondents evaluated their speaking and writing skills in either of them as mediocre or poor (see Table 4). Moreover, there was no big difference between levels of oral and written proficiency, which was reported by Hungarian-language graduates. Not surprisingly, the knowledge of the main everyday language was even better, although in this case writing lagged behind speaking as the former was mostly acquired at school where Russian got less attention than Crimean Tatar and Ukrainian. While Simferopol students could not match their peers from towns and villages in their knowledge of Crimean Tatar, they were more proficient not only in Russian but also (perhaps due to higher quality of teaching) in Ukrainian. The students' self-evaluation thus creates the impression that the Crimean Tatar schools managed to perform both the identity and integration tasks fairly well. The results of the tests the students took in the spring of 2008 confirm that the graduates of the Crimean Tatar schools had rather good knowledge of Ukrainian, as their mean scores in that language were not much lower than in other subjects, which most of them chose to take in the best-known Russian. Nor were these graduates, unlike Hungarians in Transcarpathia, hindered on the way to higher education by their scores in the Ukrainian language and literature.

However, most of the existing schools face serious problems impeding their accomplishment of this mission. To begin with, it is only in name that they are schools with the instruction in Crimean Tatar, as that language prevails only on the primary level, while in secondary school most subjects are taught in Russian, with Crimean Tatar elements at best (which is why students predominantly choose Russian for testing). As interviewed directors told me, the main obstacles to teaching in Crimean Tatar are a lack of textbooks (which are translated very slowly, mostly due to scarcity of competent people) and a lack of qualified teachers in all subjects (interviews Abibova, Akhmedov). No training of teachers for Crimean Tatar schools – other than instructors of the eponymous language and literature – has been implemented at any of the state universities, nor do Crimean Tatars have a private institution of higher education as do the Hungarians. While the former deficit has partly to do with the reluctance of the authorities, the latter is virtually predetermined by the fact that this group has no kin-state that could provide financial assistance for meeting its educational and other needs.[4] This also exacerbates other problems, such as a lack of adequate building renovation, equipment and so on.[5]

The crucial challenge to the Crimean Tatar education have been, however, a rather ambivalent attitude of the bulk of the group, with many parents reluctant to send their children to minority schools even in those localities where they are available. While some parents prefer such schools because they can give their children knowledge of the group language and culture, others take into account pragmatic factors such as the school's proximity to home, conditions of buildings, optional subjects offered and reputation of teachers. Moreover, the very fact of learning in – or even of – Crimean Tatar is often perceived as disadvantageous for children's mastering of 'essential' subjects and/or higher education and careers, in particular outside of Crimea. In schools with the instruction in Russian or Ukrainian, many Crimean Tatar parents even renounce lessons of the minority language for their children as such lessons usually take place in addition to all others or at the time when other children learn 'more important' subjects (Tyschchenko et al. 2011, 46, 76; interviews Abibova, Iaiaeva). It is clear that minority members have largely internalised majority perceptions of the value of various languages, on the one hand, and of educational values, on the other. They are ready to downplay ethnocultural difference, which might put their children at a disadvantage.

Therefore, many Crimean Tatar politicians and educators believe that, in contrast to the first years after the repatriation, the main problem of education in their group language is no longer resistance of the authorities but, rather, 'indifference' of the masses. Similarly to their Hungarian counterparts, these elites tend to prefer the interests of the 'nation' over those of individuals. Hence, they deem it necessary to more actively persuade parents of the benefits of education in Crimean Tatar or even exert some pressure on them (interviews Chubarov, Seitvelieva). Given that education in the group's language is an essential component of its cultural development, some interviewees considered appropriate to proceed to instruction of all or most subjects in Crimean Tatar, even if that led more parents to prefer mainstream schools. At the same time, they believed that it was crucially important to increase attractiveness of schools in the group language by creating opportunities to use it in various domains, for which the Ukrainian parliament should declare it one of the official languages of the Crimean autonomy (interviews Abibova, Kadzhametova). However, other interviewees considered such development unrealistic in the foreseeable future. At least for the time being, they preferred a mixed education with the expansion of the Crimean Tatar component to include all subjects in primary school and humanities on the secondary level, while keeping the state language (or rather introducing it instead of Russian) for sciences. While some considered such mixture to be appropriate only as a temporary solution under unfavorable conditions, others viewed it as the best possible option for a minority group (e.g. interviews Chubarov, Iaiaeva).

No doubt the current situation influences the views of what is realistic and appropriate, among the elites and particularly among the masses who are not fully supportive of the leaders' nationalist priorities. It is hardly surprising that the graduating students preferred teaching of most subjects in Crimean Tatar and some in Ukrainian to the exclusive use of the group language. While the former model got support from 52% of respondents, the latter was only chosen by 16% (further 26% preferred some combination of Crimean Tatar and Russian). These preferences were consistent with the fact that two thirds of respondents intended to study at a university in Russian or Ukrainian. Most parents declared similar preferences for the group education in general and their children's prospects in particular (cf. Chernyi 2005). Therefore, attempts to introduce exclusive education in Crimean Tatar would be met with an even warier reaction of parents which would further limit the popular base of such education and, accordingly, its contribution to the preservation of the group identity.

Conclusion

The above analysis has demonstrated a striking difference between the school systems for Ukraine's two minorities. Having been moulded by divergent historical contexts, they differed not only in starting conditions but also in their treatment by the authorities, economic situation and, accordingly, language regime and educational performance, which determined their ability to fulfill the tasks of forming ethnocultural identity and promoting social integration. In the Hungarian case, a favourable attitude of the Ukrainian authorities, strong support of the kin-state and, above all, a tradition and an infrastructure developed prior to Ukraine's independence contributed to the predominant instruction of the youth in their native language. This ensured the reproduction of language knowledge and identity among the minority members but perpetuated the problem of their inability to use Ukrainian in communication with the majority, which limited their nationwide mobility and led them to demand continued use of Hungarian in Transcarpathia. Although a long tradition of Hungarian-language education contributed to the readiness by the authorities to tolerate this situation, they became impatient with the minorities' limited proficiency in the state language. The implementation of a policy intended to overcome this shortcoming, albeit it did not extend beyond a language test for school graduates, put the Hungarian youth at a strong disadvantage in access to higher education. Moreover, the realisation of the importance of the state language for social mobility may urge ever more Hungarians to choose an accommodating path for their children and thus eventually hinder inter-generational reproduction of the group language and identity.

The situation of the Crimean Tatar has been much more unfavourable. Since schooling in their group language had to be created anew after their return to Crimea, it required much more money, resolution and a change of attitudes than for the Hungarians, and it could not immediately produce high-quality education that would appeal to parents choosing a school for their children. The authorities on the regional and local levels, while severely contstrained by a lack of funds, often did not even want to help Crimean Tatar returnees, viewed as endangering social stability and established cultural values. Having no kin-state, the group could not get strong support from abroad. Moreover, the realisation of the little value of the minority language for career opportunities made many parents prefer educating their children in Russian or Ukrainian. As a result, the bulk of the group's youth has been schooled in languages other than Crimean Tatar, which prevented them from mastering the latter, all the more so because they could not easily pick it up in other practices. Even in the nominally minority-language schools, the instruction in Crimean Tatar was actually limited to the primary and, in some subjects, lower secondary level. The limited use of Crimean Tatar in education exacerbated the problem of its poor knowledge by the group members and, therefore, vulnerability of their cultural identity.

The best way to solve the two groups' educational problems seems to be the introduction of bilingual schooling. Children would be instructed in the minority language at the primary level, while having an intensive communication-oriented course of Ukrainian, and then would use the latter language for ever more subjects on the secondary level when sufficient proficiency therein is achieved. This model would allow a considerable improvement in the students' knowledge of Ukrainian without endangering their learning of the minority language and culture, which should eventually make such schools appealing to most parents in the respective groups. However, if this model is imposed *instead* of the exclusive minority-language education, it may be perceived as discriminatory by many minority members, which was the problem with its attempted introduction in Ukraine in 2009 (or a similar step taken in Latvia in 2004; Hogan-Brun [2006]). Therefore, the mixed model should be launched as another option *in addition* to tracks with exclusive instruction in the official and the group language. This solution is applicable not only to those minorities with full-fledged systems of education in their group languages, such as Hungarians and Romanians, but also to those for which such systems are being created, for example, the Crimean Tatars or Bulgarians. As my analysis demonstrates, the creation has been impeded not only by shortages of funds but also by a lack of qualified teachers and, most important, by the apprehension of many parents that education in a lesser-used language would do their children more harm than good. A combination of the group and state languages would diminish all these obstacles, particularly the last one, thus allowing minority-tailored education to expand much faster than it has been done so far. This is not an ideal system for achieving both main goals of minority education, but it will enable significant progress in each direction without critical loss in the other. Of course, this conclusion is only valid if one does not embrace extreme ideals favouring the achievement of one goal to the point of completely rejecting the other, that is, integration through assimilation or preservation of identity by means of segregation.

Two main problems hinder the implementation of this proposal. The first is the widespread perception of the appropriateness of monolingual instruction in minority languages for their (willing) speakers, which was brought about by the Soviet practice of such education and reinforced by post-Soviet references to minority rights. As argued above, minority leaders insist on the inviolability of such instruction, which they see as a precondition for the reproduction of group identity. 'Rank-and-file' members are generally supportive of schooling in their native language, although they do not share the leaders' nationalist subordination of individual interests to collective ones. While many Hungarians and Crimean Tatars already prefer the use of both minority and majority languages in the educational process, it may take some time before most members of each group see it not as a loss of schooling in the group language but as the most adequate version thereof.

Another, specifically Ukrainian problem is a large discrepancy between the currency and prestige of the Russian language, on the one hand, and its legal status as just a minority language, on the other, which has been the main object of controversy in language policy. While some consider it dangerous to perpetuate a special role of the former imperial language, others do not accept the same treatment of languages with vastly different numbers of speakers and social functions. The problem is not only that for Russian, the transition to bilingual education is not expedient in those regions where its speakers constitute a solid majority and, therefore, can expect to combine identity and integration on the basis of their own language. The transition is also impeded by the political power of the representatives of these regions and the magnitude of their opposition to a policy they see as detrimental to their constituency. It is their coming to power in 2010 that led to the cancellation of the announced transition to bilingual education, and their opposition will continue to hinder the uniform application of this plan to all minorities in all regions. Therefore, the only way to proceed with such transition is to introduce a mixed system as a parallel option, which is likely to be more popular in those places where the prevalence of the titular language leads many minority members to seek better knowledge thereof and/or where exclusive education in the respective minority language is already considered inadequate. In this way, the state would respond to the citizens' preferences rather than imposing its own. Such behaviour will only be possible with the democratisation and decentralisation of Ukrainian education and governance in general, which is far from certain at the time of this writing but will remain on the political agenda as long as the elites continue to declare their European aspirations.

Acknowledgements

Research for this article was facilitated by a fellowship of the Local Government and Public Service Reform Initiative, Open Society Institute (Budapest). I am grateful to Natalia Belitser and Yuliia Tyshchenko for helping me with contacts and sources. Thanks are also due to François Vaillancourt, François Grin and two anonymous reviewers for their insightful comments on earlier drafts.

Notes

1. I calculated the mean scores of particular schools on the basis of data presented at the website of the authority administering the testing (http://www.vintest.org.ua/statistics.aspx). Each of the studied minority-language schools was compared with two majority-language ones of the same type in the same or a neighbouring locality. A macro-level analysis by Muravyev and Talavera (2010) confirms a big difference between the Hungarian- and Romanian-language schools, on the one hand, and the Ukrainian ones, on the other, in the mean scores in the Ukrainian language and literature, albeit for the 2009 and 2010 tests.
2. It is only in the late-1960s that Crimean Tatar started to be taught as a subject in many Central Asian schools where the group's children studied (interview Kadzhametova).
3. Given a scarcity of TV programs, books and periodicals in Crimean Tatar, the figures for its use in these practices, however low, are probably exaggerated, indicating not so much actual patterns as those considered appropriate for Crimean Tatars. The group loyalty might also affect other figures in this and Table 4.
4. As Turkey hosts a large Crimean Tatar diaspora, it has rendered some financial and political support for the Crimean Tatars in Ukraine. In particular, several dozen youth have been admitted annually to Turkish universities on a special quota (interview Kadzhametova). However, this training seems to be more instrumental in the cultivation of the educated elite than in providing personnel for mass domains such as school education.
5. Although a major part of funds allotted by the Ukrainian government and international organization for the integration of the former deportees went for schools, these sums were far from adequate for meeting their needs (interview Dzhemilev). Private initiatives were mostly aimed at domains other than education.

References

All-Ukrainian Population Census. n.d. Government of Ukraine. http://2001.ukrcensus.gov.ua/eng/

Allworth, E. 1998. *The Tatars of Crimea: Return to the homeland*. 2nd ed. Durham and London: Duke University Press.

Bamgbose, A. 2004. Language of instruction policy and practice in Africa. UNESCO. http://www.unesco.org/education/languages_2004/languageinstruction_africa.pdf

Bazhal, A. 2008. ZNO: Povtorennia – maty navchannia [Testing: Repetitio est mater studiorum]. *Dzerkalo tyzhnia*, February 23.

Biesta, G. 2007. The education-socialisation conundrum or 'Who is afraid of education?' *Utbilding & Demokrati* 16, no. 3: 25–36.

Bilaniuk, L., and S. Melnyk. 2008. A tense and shifting balance. Bilingualism and education in Ukraine. *International Journal of Bilingual Education and Bilingualism* 11, no. 3–4: 340–72.

Burger, H. 2003. Language rights and linguistic justice in the education system of the Habsburg Monarchy. Istituto per gli Incontri Culturali Mitteleuropei. http://www.incontrimitteleuropei.it/english/papers.asp?li=eng

Chernychko, S. 2009. Napriamky movnoï osvity Ukraïny i uhors'komovna osvita na Zakarpatti [Trends in language education in Ukraine and the Hungarian-language education in Transcarpathia]. *Acta Beregsasiensis* VIII, no. 2: 97–106.

Chernyi, E.V. 2005. Issledovanie vospriiatiia modelei obrazovaniia naseleniem poli-kul'turnogo regiona [A study of the perception of education models by the population of a multicultural region]. In *Mezhetnicheskie otnosheniia v Krymu: Poisk putei rannego preduprezhdeniia konfliktnykh situatsii...* [Interethnic relations in Crimea: A search for ways of an early prevention of conflict situations...], ed. M.A. Aradzhioni, 13–32. Simferopol: Sonat. www.ciet.org.ua/docs/sbornik/p_13-32_cherniy.doc

Chilachava, R., and T. Pylypenko. 2004. Deiaki aspekty realizatsiï derzhavnoï polit-yky u sferi mizhnatsional'nykh vidnosyn Ukraïny [Some aspects of the implementation of the state policy regarding interethnic relations in Ukraine]. In *Mizhnatsional'ni vidnosyny i natsional'ni menshyny Ukraïny* [Interethnic relations and national minorities of Ukraine], ed. R. Chilachava, 160–84. Kyiv: Holovna spetsializovana redaktsiia literatury movamy natsional'nykh menshyn Ukraïny.

Ciscel, M.H. 2008. Uneasy compromise: Language and education in Moldova. *International Journal of Bilingual Education and Bilingualism* 11, no. 3–4: 373–95.

Concept of education in the Crimean Tatar language in the Autonomous Republic of Crimea. 2007. *Tasil*, no. 1: 49–60.

Cummins, J. 1989. *Empowering minority students.* Sacramento: Association of Bilingual Education.

European Commission against Racism and Intolerance. 2011. ECRI Report on Ukraine (fourth monitoring cycle). ECRI. http://www.coe.int/t/dghl/monitoring/ecri/Country-by-country/Ukraine/UKR-CbC-IV-2012-006-ENG.pdf

Gibson, M.A. 1993. The school performance of immigrant minorities: A comparative view. In *Minority education: Anthropological perspectives*, ed. E. Jacob and C. Jordan, 113–28. Norwood, NJ: Ablex.

Hogan-Brun, G. 2006. At the interface of language ideology and practice. The public discourse surrounding the 2004 education reform in Latvia. *Language Policy* 5, no. 3: 313–33.

Izuchenie gosudarstvennogo iazyka, organizatsiia obucheniia na nem [The learning of the state language and the organization of instruction therein]. n.d. Unpublished document of the Ministry of Education and Science of the Autonomous Republic of Crimea.

Janmaat, J.G. 2000. *Nation-building in post-Soviet Ukraine: Educational policy and the response of the Russian-speaking population.* Amsterdam: University of Amsterdam.

Kalynovs'ka, O. 2009. Language situation in education. In *Language policy and language situation in Ukraine: Analysis and recommendation*, ed. J. Besters-Dilger, 201–41. Frankfurt am Main: Peter Lang.

Kulyk, V. 2009. Language policies and language attitudes in post-Orange Ukraine. In *Language policy and language situation in Ukraine: Analysis and recommendation*, ed. J. Besters-Dilger, 15–55. Frankfurt am Main: Peter Lang.

Martin, T. 2001. *The affirmative action empire: Nations and nationalism in the Soviet Union, 1923–1939.* Ithaca and London: Cornell University Press.

Martin-Jones, M., and M. Heller. 1996. Introduction to the special issues on education in multilingual settings: Discourse, identities and power. *Linguistics and Education* 8, no. 2: 127–37.

Meyer, J.W. 1977. The effects of education as an institution. *American Journal of Sociology* 83, no. 1: 55–77.

Muravyev, A., and O. Talavera. 2010. Can state language policies distort students' demand for higher education? Discussion paper No. 5411, Institute for the Study of Labour.

Pavlenko, A. 2011. Language rights versus speakers' rights: On the applicability of Western language rights approaches in Eastern European contexts. *Language Policy* 10, no. 1: 37–58.

Polese, A. 2010. The formal and the informal: Exploring 'Ukrainian' education in Ukraine, scenes from Odessa. *Comparative Education* 46, no. 1: 47–62.

Riabchun, Y. 2010. Dmitrii Tabachnik uchit novomu [Dmytro Tabachnyk teaches the new]. *Kommersant-Ukraina*, March 26. http://www.kommersant.ua/doc.html?DocID=1343216&IssueId=7000402

Søvik, M.B. 2007. *Support, resistance and pragmatism: An examination of motivation in language policy in Kharkiv, Ukraine.* Stockholm: Stockholm University.

Stepanenko, V. 1999. *The construction of identity and school policy in Ukraine.* Commack: Nova Science Publishers.

Stewart, S. 2005. *Explaining the low intensity of ethnopolitical conflict in Ukraine.* Münster: LIT.

Szilágyi, L. 2009. Language learning strategies used by monolingual and bilingual students in Transcarpathian secondary schools. *Acta Beregsasiensis* VIII, no. 2: 163–76.

Thomas, R.K., and A.L. Wahrhaftig. 1971. Indians, hillbillies and the 'education problem'. In *Anthropological perspectives on education*, ed. M.L. Wax, S. Diamond, and F.O. Gearing, 230–51. New York: Basic Books.

Tyshchenko, Y.A. et al. 2011. *Rivnyi dostup do iakisnoï osvity v AR Krym: Vyklyky i perspektyvy v polikul'turnomu rehioni* [Equal access to quality education in the Autonomous Republic of Crimea: Challenges and prospects in a multicultural region]. Kyiv: Ahentstvo 'Ukraïna'. http://www.ucipr.kiev.ua/files/books/crimea_education2011.pdf

U shkolakh iz movoiu natsmenshyn posyliat' vyvchennia ukraïns'koï [The teaching of Ukrainian in national minority schools will be strengthened]. 2008. *Novynar*, May 28. Novynar. http://novynar.com.ua/politics/28182

Vardy, S.B. 1989. Soviet nationality policy in Carpatho-Ukraine since World War II: The Hungarians of sub-Carpathia. *Hungarian Studies Review* XVI, no. 1–2: 67–91.

Zadovolennia osvitnikh zapytiv natsional'nykh menshyn Zakarpattia [Meeting educational demands of the national minorities of Transcarpathia]. n.d. Unpublished electronic document of the Transcarpathian regional state administration.

Appendix. List of the author's interviews

Transcarpathia

Arpa, Petro, director of school no. 10 in the city of Uzhhorod. Uzhhorod, 15 February 2008.

Bubniak, Mariia, head of the education department of the Berehove municipal state administration. Berehove, 12 February 2008.

Hertsoh, Yurii, head of the education department of the Transcarpathian provincial state administration. Uzhhorod, 15 February 2008.

Kovach, Mykola, head of the Party of the Hungarians of Ukraine. Berehove, 13 February 2008.

Lendiel, Vasyl', head of the education department of the Berehove district state administration. Berehove, 13 February 2008.

Medvid', Stepan, head of the Berehove district employment center. Berehove, 14 February 2008.

Mitskyk, Yuliana, director of the school no. 4 in the town of Berehove. Berehove, 12 February 2008.

Oros, Karl, director of the school in the village of Dertsen, Mukacheve district. Dertsen, 12 February 2008.

Crimea

Abibova, El'mira, director of the school No. 2 in the village of Zuia, Bilohors'k district. Zuia, 16 May 2008.

Akhmedov, Nariman, director of the school No. 42 in the city of Simferopol. Simferopol, 12 May 2008.

Chubarov, Refat, deputy head of the Mejlis of the Crimean Tatar people. Simferopol, 14 May 2008.

Dzemilev, Mustafa, head of the Mejlis of the Crimean Tatar people. Simferopol, 12 May 2008.

Iaiaeva, Alime, main specialist at the sector for the education in the Crimean Tatar language, Ministry of Education and Science of the Autonomous Republic of Crimea. Simferopol, 16 May 2008.

Kadzhametova, Safure, head of the Association of Crimean Tatar educators 'Maarifchi'. Simferopol, 14 May 2008.

Pekhar, Halyna, head of the education department of the Bakhchysarai district state administration. Bakhchysarai, 13 May 2008.

Seitvelieva, Diliara, head of the Council of teachers of Bakhchysarai district. Bakhchysarai, 13 May 2008.

The contribution of the diaspora to the reconstruction of education in South Sudan: the challenge of being involved from a distance

Josje van der Linden, Marit Blaak and Florence Aate Andrew

Department of Lifelong Learning, Faculty of Social and Behavioural Sciences, University of Groningen, Groningen, The Netherlands

Conflicts all over the world result in people living in diaspora, usually maintaining strong ties with their countries of origin. As many of them are well educated and dedicated to their country, expectations of the role they can play in the development of their home country are high. This article reflects on the contribution of the South Sudanese diaspora to the reconstruction of the education system, which was badly affected by over 40 years of civil war. Theories of capacity development, human capabilities and transnationalism are used to build a framework to analyse micro-development projects in the education sector initiated by the South Sudanese diaspora. Case studies and in-depth interviews led to the identification of opportunities and challenges as experienced in these projects. The conclusion points to the need to rethink partnerships in the reconstruction of the education sector in South Sudan.

Introduction

In May 2012, a picture of South Sudanese refugees (Internally Displaced Persons) travelling by boat from North to South appeared in one of the Dutch newspapers (Broere 2012). The boat was packed with young adults, all of them male, standing upright and looking into the distance. The title of the article accompanying the picture, read: 'Better life in free South Sudan remains an empty promise after one year'. One of the reasons given was: 'Jobs are given to ex-combatants who have not received any education. Well educated youth from the diaspora have no chance and hardly contribute to the reconstruction of their country of birth' (Broere 2012, 17, our translation). The news article reflects the topicality of the dynamics of diaspora involvement in the reconstruction of the education sector in South Sudan addressed in this article.

From 1955 onwards, there was a civil war between North and South Sudan, interrupted by a decade of relative peace after the Addis Ababa Peace agreement was signed in 1972. The second phase of the war lasted until 2005, when the Comprehensive Peace Agreement was signed. In July 2011, South Sudan became an independent country. Most of the children who grew up during the war missed out on an education (Lako, Van der Linden, and Deng 2010). As a result, recent population statistics show a literacy rate of only 27% for the population aged 15 years and above, 40% for men and an alarming 16% for women (NBS 2012).

School attendance and violent conflicts are strongly interrelated. Violent conflicts force children to leave school at an early age. And those out of the school system are easy targets for army recruitment (Angucia 2010; Breidlid 2010; Deng 2006). In South Sudan, the conflict between North and South forced a great number of young people to leave their country. Some walked for hundreds of miles in an attempt to escape the violence around them. The strongest of these 'lost boys' made it to Uganda, Ethiopia, Kenya and, finally, to the USA or other Western countries (see the story of Valentino Achak Deng in Eggers [2006], also mentioned in UNESCO [2011]). They joined the diaspora, witnessing the independence of their country from a distance and, according to the news article cited, got hardly any chance to help in the rebuilding of their country (see also Walzer 2008).

This article explores the phenomenon discussed in the news article from the perspective of the diaspora, focusing on the education sector. The lead question is: What opportunities and challenges do the South Sudanese diaspora meet in their efforts to contribute to the reconstruction of the educational sector in their country, and how can they be partners in developing this sector?

Below, we explore the concepts of capacity development and human capabilities, while transnationalism will serve to position the diaspora as a phenomenon in a broader development perspective. We then consider the challenges and barriers for the reconstruction of the South Sudanese education system that have been identified in previous studies in the framework of the Early School Leaving in Africa Project[1] (Zeelen et al. 2010). The research methodology and main findings will be discussed, finally leading to rethinking partnerships in the reconstruction of education in South Sudan.

Partnerships, capacity development and human capabilities

Following recent trends in development theories, local ownership, agency and human capabilities are concepts that have become the main focus in development strategies. Capacity development is defined as, 'the process by which individuals, organisations, and societies develop abilities to perform functions, solve problems, set and achieve goals over time' (UNDP 2009a, 5). Strong partnerships imply capacity development to enable local stakeholders to take control over their development and to absorb other technical and financial support.

Although many organisations have acknowledged the importance of capacity development, its implementation still does not seem to be leading to sustainable local capacity (OECD 2006). In a study of best practices in capacity development, the Organisation for Economic Co-operation and Development described lack of contextualisation as the main pitfall in implementation. The study concluded that capacity development is, 'a nec-essarily endogenous process of unleashing, strengthening, creating and maintaining capacity over time' (39). Ownership, choice and self-esteem are vital values to processes of capacity development. Discussing their experiences in southern Africa, Zeelen and Van der Linden (2009) state that contextualisation, social learning and interactive knowledge production are pre-requisites for these values.

The concept of human capabilities as presented by Sen (1999) and Nussbaum (2011) gives insight into the human capability to be an agent of development through a wide range of skills, freedom and mindsets. While Sen explains how capabilities serve individuals as well as organisations and nations, Nussbaum elaborates the importance of capabilities for each human being to lead a life worthy of human dignity. Capacity development should create and sustain capabilities in order for people to be able to organise their own development within the environment in which they live. Although capacity development is an urgent need in fragile states, the context makes it hard to implement capacity development programmes. The capacity to build on is limited, as there is little trust and social capital (Brinkerhoff 2010; USAID 2010). Because of their education, their experiences and their connection to their home countries, diaspora communities should be excellent partners for this type of capacity development, as is often assumed in diaspora involvement programmes (see, for example, Ionescu 2006; Newland 2004; Obamba 2013; OECD 2010; UNDP 2009a).

The diaspora, their resources and transnationalism

While the definition of diaspora can be determined by indicators such as citizenship, length of stay, feelings of identity, perceptions and trust, this article adopts Ionescu's (2006) flexible definition of diaspora: 'members of ethnic and national communities, who have left, but maintain links with their homelands' (13). According to Faist (2010), the concept of diaspora is commonly used to indicate 'religious or national groups living outside an (imagined) homeland' and the concept of transnationalism to refer to 'migrants' durable ties across countries' (9). Because of their potential for social change and agency in a transforming world, Faist tried to bring together the two 'awkward dance partners' (9), as he called them. The edited collection *Diaspora and Transnationalism* (Bauböck and Faist 2010) discussed the two concepts as related but not interchangeable. Reviewing the literature (Bauböck and Faist 2010; Faist 2010; Guo 2013; Vertovec 2009, 2010), we conceive transnationalism as the social phenomenon that comes with migration and mobility, increased communication possibilities, and results in 'sustained cross-border relationships, patterns of exchange, affiliations and social formations spanning nation-states' as Vertovec (2009, 2) puts it. The concept of diaspora can be understood as the people living the social phenomenon of transnationalism – they are agents with experiences, feelings and plans.

The position of diaspora is often characterised by their knowledge of local needs, cultural awareness and language, as well as their commitment and loyalty to their home country (Newland 2004; Oucho 2009; Van Naersen, Kusters, and Schapendonk 2006). The African Diaspora Policy Centre (2008) added the unique value of their networks, accumulative experiences and insights. Ionescu (2006) summarised the different types of resources diaspora could contribute in homeland development as follows: human capital, financial and entrepreneurial capital, social capital, and affective and local capital. These different types of capital indicate the unique capabilities that the diaspora possess by virtue of their familiarity with home and host countries. Pre-eminently, they are the ones who know how to support their people in developing their capabilities. The main feature in their resources is related to their transnational background – a background of both local and global knowledge and experience. Likewise, the UNDP (2009b) report on *Overcoming Barriers: Human Mobility and Development* stressed the gains of mobility for human development.

From a transnational point of view, migration is not a singular journey but an integral part of life, which causes the disappearance of the distinctions between home and host country, origin and destiny, sending and receiving countries. Measures for structural inclusion like legal status, voting rights, dual citizenship and free movement should support this development (DRCMGP 2009; Ionescu 2006; Newland 2004). Besides structural inclusion, Ionescu (2006) also recommended symbolic inclusion, acknowledging diaspora's local grassroots knowledge. In the long term, this could lead to a globally shared cosmopolitan future (Vertovec 2009). As this future has not materialised yet, we will continue to refer to home and host countries.

Diaspora involvement in development

Diaspora members contribute in different ways to the development of their home countries. First, and by far the most discussed type of diaspora involvement, is the transfer of financial remittances, investment and business enhancement. The influence of remittances is highly acknowledged as they constitute a major source of external capital for developing countries (DRCMGP 2009; Ionescu 2006; Mohamoud 2006; Newland 2004; Oucho

2009). Besides financial and entrepreneurial capital, diaspora also share their human, social and local capital (ADPC 2008; Ionescu 2006; Newland 2004; OECD 2010). This means that diaspora share knowledge accumulated in their host countries with communities in home countries (OECD 2010; Sinatti 2012). Using their local capital, they influence role models, gender roles and demographic and familial behaviours and perceptions of successful life. Moreover, they can assist new governments in drafting treaties, agreements and constitutions (Mohamoud 2006). To conclude, diaspora affective capital leads to contributions, not only in the home country but also in the host country, by providing a platform for promotion of their culture and advocacy (Newland 2004; see also Diaspora Forum for Development in the Netherlands [www.d-f-d.org]). Combining the different forms of capital, many diaspora members have initiated micro-development projects, mostly targeting their home communities at the local and sub-national levels (ADPC 2008; Ionescu 2006; Mohamoud 2006; Newland 2004).

In spite of all the resources and subsequent expectations, the reality on the ground shows that not all activities fit easily into the programmes of the receiving communities. The agendas of the diaspora are not always consistent with the agendas of the population of the home country (DRCMGP 2009). Besides failing to identify local needs, some diaspora members lack the capacity to successfully implement projects, some of which are isolated efforts and lack a long-term strategic vision. Returning diaspora members find it hard to re-adjust to local norms, as local counterparts often have poor infrastructure, weak administrative, financial and technical capacity and sometimes show resentment to national expatriates (MPI 2003, as cited in Ionescu 2006; OECD 2010). Diaspora involvement is influenced by trust, which should be built up as many diaspora members suffer from feelings of suspicion, resentment, stigmatisation or even discrimination against them (Ionescu 2006; Newland 2004). Newland (2004) stressed that, 'Diaspora communities often reproduce the divisions of class, ethnicity, religion, political affiliation, language, and region that are found in their countries of origin' (v). In all this, local ownership remains of paramount importance. Initiatives are usually successful when they are led by local demand, achieve observable results, are professionally organised and match the diaspora's expertise (Van Naerssen, Kusters, and Schapendonk 2006). In relation to education, UNESCO propagated the building of partnerships between private organisations and other stakeholders in the Education for All campaign to optimise the effect of private funding and activities (OECD 2010, 2012).

De Haas and Rodriguez (2010) stated that concrete case studies are needed to understand how development and migration interact in particular contexts (see also De Haas 2005, 2010; Kleist 2008a, 2008b). This is why the focus of this article is on micro-development projects. In micro-development projects there is no personal return on investment, activities are usually small scale and vary from short-term to organised and durable efforts (Newland 2004). Moreover, micro-development projects reflect the different types of capital the diaspora possess (Ionescu 2006) and provide insight into the ability and possibilities to make use of this capital. A study among migrant organisations in the Netherlands found that most of the diaspora-initiated micro-projects relate to education, health and micro-economic activities reaching dozens to hundreds of people (van Naerssen, Kusters, and Schapendonk 2006). Mohamoud (2006) established that the impact of such activities goes beyond the direct beneficiaries as they have a broader impact on peace and political stability in the homeland. In many cases these types of projects are organised by migrant organisations based in host countries, in cooperation with local counterparts in home countries. Micro-development projects are sometimes funded through partnerships with other non-governmental organisations (NGOs) or through private foundations, but overall structural funding is lacking (Van Naerssen, Kusters, and Schapendonk 2006). The progress of these projects shows how diaspora and local partners interact and negotiate in practice and reveals the dynamics of migration and development in their context. Besides this, the case studies give insight into the educational challenges in South Sudan and the diaspora's perspective on the way forward.

Reconstructing education in South Sudan

Although the war in South Sudan ended in 2005, and independence from North Sudan was gained in 2011, access to basic education is still a considerable challenge in this new country. The General Education Strategic Plan (2012–2017) declares that its context is:

> not only challenging, it is daunting. Decades of neglect and years of civil war have left the country with a shattered infrastructure, a large diaspora of some of its best talents, and generations of youth who never had the opportunity to attend school. (MGEI 2012, 13)

The Education for All Global Monitoring Report for South Sudan declared that the education system in South Sudan is, 'close to the bottom of the global league table for educational opportunity, especially for young girls' (UNESCO 2011, 1). While the delivery of basic services, like education, should be a peace dividend, the reality is still grim. People are re-migrating from North Sudan and neighbouring countries to South Sudan. Many young people need education and training. A total of 58% of the population in South Sudan is less than 20 years old (NBS 2012). At the moment education is mainly provided through donors and international agencies and NGOs, which, to a great extent, fail to provide flexible solutions (UNESCO 2011). Yet the long-term vision of the Republic of South Sudan is to build 'an educated and informed nation' by 2040 (Kiir Mayardit 2011, 1).

Previous studies of the Early School Leaving in Africa project (Zeelen et al. 2010) identified the barriers to rebuilding the educational system in South Sudan as: political barriers, poverty-related barriers, culture as a barrier to education and barriers related to the quality of education (Lako, Van der Linden, and Deng 2010; see also Sommers 2005). The political barriers relate to the history of Sudan, where the North dominated the South and took the benefits of its rich resources like the oil revenues. The political domination by the North is also reflected in the imposition of Arabic as the language of instruction and in a curriculum biased towards Arabic culture and history, neglecting South Sudanese history, traditions and culture (Breidlid 2005, 2010). Regarding poverty, Deng (2006) explains that the gaps in the development of South Sudan originate from the British colonisation before the war. These gaps contributed greatly to the neglect of education and other parental priorities (Ibrahim 2008). Education became a less urgent priority than the short-term requirement to maintain livelihoods. Generally, boys were given priority over girls when it came to attending school. In livestock-owning communities with a semi-nomadic lifestyle, culture formed a barrier to formal education as parents preferred their children to learn informally while working (Van Beurden 2006 [see also Farag (2012), who studied this phenomenon in Kordofan province]). In spite of all this, some communities managed to maintain schools, sometimes supported by NGOs. These schools operated in a rather isolated way (Sommers 2005) and support by NGOs was fragmented (UNESCO 2011).

The Global Monitoring Report on Education for All (UNESCO 2012) drew attention to the oil-wealth of the country as a potential means for building an education system. The report identified capacity constraints as the main barrier to the expansion of the system. The priorities of the Ministry of General Education and Instruction include: promoting adult literacy, building institutional and human capacity and promoting partnerships among stakeholders (MGEI 2012). According to the ministry, significant emphasis is given to improving quality. Two major issues are threatening the quality of education in South Sudan: the implementation of the new curriculum and qualified teachers. Without the necessary teaching materials and teacher training, the implementation of the South Sudanese curriculum remains a big challenge and schools refer to the curriculum of neighbouring countries instead (Deng 2006). Second, basic working conditions and low salaries are unlikely to attract trained teachers, especially in rural areas. Facing the immense challenges ahead, the education sector needs partnerships at different levels to improve the situation (Lako, Van der Linden, and Deng 2010; NGO Forum Southern Sudan 2009; see also Bieckmann 2012). To face capacity limitations, the Government of South Sudan (GoSS 2011) speaks of, 'a continued effort to attract the diaspora and to train existing staff to enhance capacity' (xxii), thus stressing the potential of the diaspora.

UNESCO (2011) also refers to the potential of diaspora, proposing a results-oriented pooled fund to avoid fragmentation.

The concepts discussed point to three key issues for this research. First, theories on capacity development and human capabilities draw our attention to the resources of the members of the diaspora. Secondly, transnationalism builds on this and adds the perspective of increased mobility around the world. Thirdly, the challenges of the education system make us wonder how the diaspora set their priorities and how they engage in partnerships with the government and other stakeholders.

Research into diaspora involvement in development

The aim of our research was to analyse the opportunities and challenges faced by diaspora development initiatives to contribute to the reconstruction of education in South Sudan and to reflect on ways for partnership cooperation in this sector. Studying pro-active and creative forms of diaspora involvement in the form of micro-development projects would provide insights into the day-to-day challenges of diaspora members trying to make a change. Qualitative research revealed not only the experiences of the diaspora in executing their activities, but also the ways in which they evaluate these experiences (Flick 2006; Hennink, Hutter, and Bailey 2010).

To get an overview of the ways in which diaspora members are encouraged and received in South Sudan upon their return, we made an inventory of existing policies, practices and problems involving the diaspora in South Sudan. This was done through the study of policy documents, papers and NGO reports. To explore the perceptions and initiatives of the South Sudanese diaspora living in the Netherlands towards rebuilding education, we used participant observation, attending seminars, meetings and celebrations of the South Sudanese diaspora in the Netherlands. In this way we got to know different diaspora activities and we established contacts and trust, which enabled us to conduct in-depth interviews with active diaspora members. Three micro-development projects were identified to be followed more closely by way of a tracer study. The first is still in its starting phase, the second project has considerable working experience in northern Sudan and has now moved to the South, and the third project was established some years ago in northern Uganda and has recently started working in South Sudan.

The projects were chosen because of their different perspectives on education. Furthermore, it was expected that the different phases of conception and implementation would give an insight into the interaction between development and migration on the ground. In each case, semi-structured interviews with the main initiators of the projects[2] were conducted. Information from the interviews was enriched by field reports and documents to gain an in-depth view of the progress of the projects and the challenges experienced. Sharing the experiences in the three projects provided the opportunity to get an understanding of the challenges on the ground. The findings presented below mainly reflect the experiences and reflections of the diaspora in their expatriate position. An exploratory field visit to South Sudan gave a first insight into the views of the receiving development partners. The next field visit to South Sudan will add to this, leading to a more nuanced view of the interaction between diaspora and the local community, grounding the theory on migration and development in the realities as experienced (Baarda, De Goede, and Teunissen 2009; Creswell 2007).

Initiatives to support diaspora involvement in the development of South Sudan

The GoSS expressed great interest in involving professionals from the diaspora in public service, in order to 'Sudanise' employment. In 2007, the Minister of Regional Coordination emphasised a specific need for diaspora support in the decentralisation of governance, which resulted in the establishment of a directorate in charge of diaspora issues in the Ministry of Regional Cooperation (GoSS 2005; USAID 2009b). Several programmes ran to use the diaspora's skills for (government) employment and diaspora members have legal rights such as dual citizenship and participation in elections and referendums (Njoka 2007; USAID 2009c).

Although the programmes provided quite a number of diaspora members with opportunities to share their knowledge with local counterparts, USAID (2009a) concluded their feasibility study for a second phase of Diaspora Skills Transfer Programme, a return programme in the education sector, with strong doubts. Reasons not to return to South Sudan were commitments, such as student loans and family responsibilities, and constraints related to the situation in South Sudan, such as access to quality education, healthcare and security (see also Ionescu 2006; OECD 2010). On the organisational side, diaspora members often encountered problems adjusting to an under-functioning administrative culture. These experiences are in line with constraints in previous studies discussed (see for example, Ionescu 2006) and make us wonder whether micro-development projects in education encounter similar opportunities and challenges for the involvement of the diaspora.

South Sudanese diaspora and the reconstruction of education

The year 2011 was a turbulent one for South Sudan and also for South Sudanese living in the Netherlands. In January 2011, the South Sudanese voted for secession from the North and in July their independence was a fact. In the Netherlands this was reflected in meetings and discussions organised by a variety of stakeholders, both South Sudanese and Dutch[3]. Apart from the general situation of South Sudan and the perspectives for development, the contribution of the South Sudanese to the development of their country came to the fore. The documentary *Hinterland*, for example, shows how former child soldier Kon Kelei graduated in international law, managed to raise money and returned to South Sudan to teach law and to build a secondary school in his home town Cuey Machar (www.cmsf.nl). One of the diaspora members interviewed, stated:

> This is a must for the country. It has to prioritise public services in order to be able to establish the institutions which are the backbone for the nation building because an educated and healthy work force is necessary for the development of sustainable livelihoods. ... Last year I made a proposal to open a school, a secondary school in Jonglei state. The idea of having such a school is to have a boarding school for various tribes in the region, to provide them with good education, giving them that culture of living in peace and accepting each other. (David Chau, August 2012)

After independence, the two major issues for South Sudanese living in the Netherlands were their involvement in the development of their home country and their personal decision to return to their country or not. Interviews and conversations with members of the diaspora reveal how education plays an important role in both these issues: the state of education in South Sudan is a challenge for interventions, but securing a good education for their own children is a reason not to return to South Sudan.

Three micro-development projects in education

We turn now to consider three micro-development projects in the education sector – one that offers support to primary education, another that aims to provide education and housing for street children and a third that develops vocational training for women and youth. They are three among many other projects (UNESCO 2011) supporting the reconstruction of the education sector in South Sudan. The overview in Table 1 summarises details on the founders, the aims, the motivations, the stages and the funding (derived from project documents and interviews).

Before describing the opportunities and challenges facing these three projects, we supplement the information in Table 1 with some background information on the motivation and experiences of the three project founders (derived from interviews).

The first project, *Supporting Primary Education*, was deeply influenced by the personal history of its initiators:

> When the war came, we in the villages became the victims. Because of lack of education we were easily manipulated to join the army. So it is best to educate these villages, so they are aware of what is going on in the whole country. (Bol Deng, May 2011)

Table 1. Overview of the three micro-development projects discussed.

Case	Supporting Primary Education	Education and home for street children	Vocational training for women and youth
Founders	Two male students, refugees, living in the Netherlands	Female refugee, living with her family in the Netherlands	Female refugee (health reasons), grown-up son in South Sudan
Aim	To rebuild a school for primary education in Bor region	To provide shelter and education for street children in Wau	To train women and youth in vocational and life skills for self-sustenance in northern Uganda
Motivation	To prevent manipulation of children becoming child soldiers	To support the children to be able to help themselves and others	To support a women and youth Community Based Organisation
Stage	Planning and fund-raising phase	Planning and fund-raising phase in South Sudan (activities already carried out in North Sudan)	Centre is established; sustainability is a challenge; expansion to activities in South Sudan
Funding	Private sponsors	Private sponsors, Church	Private sponsors, Church, Dutch NGOs

In spite of this strong motivation, the project had not yet started. After our first meeting in May 2011, Bol Deng paid a visit to South Sudan. Family matters kept him from initiating his project. He returned to the Netherlands to study for his Master's degree, but later decided to break off to return to South Sudan permanently. There, he found the school he wanted to support further dilapidated by the rains.

The founder Ibtisam Aymen of the second project, *Education and Home for Street Children*, saw an important role for education:

> During the war we started in North Sudan, in Khartoum. Southerners who fled the war in the South, were living in camps around Khartoum in very bad conditions. We had a financial adoption scheme for children in those camps to provide them with food, education and healthcare. Some of them made it to university with our help. Now we are moving to the South. I come from Wau. When I visited my home town some years ago I saw many street children. We want to build an orphanage for the smaller children and let them go to school. … We have to look to the future. The new generation should be prepared for the future. Education is important. It makes people independent. They can help themselves and others. (Ibtisam Aymen, June 2011, our translation)

In spite of the visit she paid to the project area in February 2012, Ibtisam did not succeed in starting her project because she did not manage to get her piece of land registered. She connected this disappointing experience to the post-conflict situation of the country: 'Look, the country is new and the system there is complicated' (Ibtisam Aymen, August 2012, our translation).

The third project *Vocational Training for Women and Youth* seemed to have a more pragmatic vision on the role of education. Amy Flynn whom we interviewed followed an appeal by an already existing group:

> We started by supporting the Sudanese refugee orphans who were living in the camps or at home in northern Uganda, in vocational training. We managed to support about 15 students in vocational training, both girls and boys in car mechanics, electricity, carpentry, and bricklaying and construction work. When I went there in 2003, I met a group of women who were organised, but did not have a place to do their activities. They were selling groundnuts, oil and other food products in the open market. Most of them went for literacy classes, because they were illiterate. So we decided to build a vocational training centre for women and youth in northern Uganda. (Amy Flynn, May 2011)

The three projects reflect the general characteristics of diaspora development projects as identified by Van Naerssen, Kusters, and Schapendonk (2006). *The Vocational Training Centre for Women and Youth* was the only one of the three projects that already had a considerable history. When South Sudan was a war zone, the project started in northern Uganda to support Sudanese refugees and the surrounding community. The founder, Amy, stressed the importance of a strong group on the ground consisting of women and youth, who are the owners of the project. This came close to ownership as a success factor for capacity development (OECD 2006). Following the first interview, Amy also visited the project locations. She commented: 'The only worry and challenge now, is the sustainability of the centre. ... If they could get a visionary leader or an experienced development worker, I think the centre could rise to a higher level.' Amy's foundation has now expanded its activities to a health centre and a nursery school in South Sudan, also in cooperation with active communities.

Opportunities and challenges for diaspora micro-development projects

Regarding opportunities, the discussion of theories on capacity development and capabilities raised expectations to find capabilities for the implementation of capacity development and partnership in the members of the diaspora. Indeed, the three founders of the development projects displayed their strong Involvement and context knowledge of their home regions. Bol for example viewed his project as a kind of compensation:

> The war distorted us, set many families outside, disconnected all the families. The peace will now reunite them back again, we will focus. I had a bad experience, but now the experience that I have, good positive ones I want to bring them back, to compensate for the bad experience that I had before. (Bol Deng, May 2011)

Ibtisam reiterated: 'Yes, I am from Wau and for me it is easier to start something there, to get into contact with people and to build the project.' Although Amy's project was not situated in the town where she was born, her contacts in the region led her to identify active groups of people: 'It is easy to use already established structures or organised groups on the ground. … We are just a bridge between the donors and groups in the South, who really need help.' Local knowledge and social and family ties in the home country gave easy access to responsible people in the community and to cooperation with local organisations, even going beyond family ties. In line with Ionescu's (2006) term *local capital*, the strong ties with the home region were an asset for the projects.

Ibtisam's position in the diaspora was also an advantage: 'Yes, our being here has a purpose: to help people here and to do something there at the same time. While I am here, I am, so to say, the source of the work there.' She said this with some hesitation though: 'We as people in the West are able to do something there, but, who knows, if there will come a time when we will go there.' In the host country, the founders of the projects learned new skills and gained new insights, which they wanted to share. Also, they were part of new networks in churches, neighbourhoods, schools and social media, which gave them the opportunity to raise funds. The words of Bol ('bring back'), Amy ('bridge') and Ibtisam ('source') refer to their transnational position. Although they combine capabilities from different backgrounds, the words also show that the distinction between home and host country had not disappeared as theories on transnationalism suggest (compare Faist 2010; Guo 2013; Vertovec 2009, 2010).

When it comes to discussing the challenges for diaspora micro-development projects, it is important to notice that none of the three projects was firmly established in South Sudan. We observed the same situation in education projects of other diaspora members: they were either still in the phase of planning or in a rudimentary phase. What was keeping them from moving ahead? Previous studies pointed to different views about the needs on the ground (DRCMGP 2009). In South Sudan, we found these needs to be so overwhelming that any help fell short. Bol Deng described the enormous task ahead as follows:

> So we really need to do a lot as diaspora to support the people on the ground there. Because many things, they are in need of everything, clean water, they need medical treatment; they need houses to be built, roads construction, housing and schools. But education is the first important priority in the country. (Bol Deng, May 2011)

Ibtisam stressed how little an organisation can do compared to the needs in South Sudan: 'It is not easy to help everybody. If you can only help two, three or five people, then that is also good. Because the country is big and the need is very high.'

One year later, emerging tribal conflicts caused persistent feelings of insecurity and discrimination. According to Bol, people who were in power were excluding others: 'So a monopoly is going somewhere around those who take the power … it is not good, it is very dangerous.' Alongside the emerging conflicts at the border with Sudan and volatile negotiations on oil revenues, these are characteristics of the post-conflict situation of South Sudan (see also GoSS 2011; MGEI 2012). The limited capacities of the local community also related to this situation:

> The problem is the distance. You can get into contact with them, but the African way: they talk nicely on the telephone, but they never send a report. And here in the West, without a report you do not get support. That is really a big problem. … People have to learn to work administratively, and make plans. That is the problem … maybe because of the war, the long lasting war, when they only thought about fleeing and taking care of their families. This has to be developed in the people. They have to learn. (Ibtisam Aymen, June 2011, our translation)

It seems that diaspora members feel the urge to act, confronted with the post-conflict situation of their country. Since the needs are enormous, they resort to micro-development projects, but even for these projects, it is difficult to get started. Is this the way to rebuild the educational system? Below we consider the different perspectives on education taken by each of these projects.

Perspectives on education

When talking about the *Supporting Primary Education* project, Bol Deng stressed the importance of education for peace building to promote independent thinking and prevent manipulation:

> In Africa children are taught just to copy what the teacher explains to them. In Holland, there is always a debate in the class. Children learn an independent way of thinking, interpreting what they are learning. That is what we have to train the teachers. (Bol Deng, May 2011)

However, a year later, he referred to tribal clashes, stating: 'We have to build a country. We should not think about this is Dinka. This is … that way of thinking has to go' (August 2012). Just as Breidlid (2010) wanted school to play a role in correcting biased attributions between North and South Sudan, school may also play a role in combating tribalism in the South. Ibtisam thought education alone would not provide the right learning environment for children and youth. For example, she criticised one of the international NGOs thus:

> They have a beautiful school. The children go there every day, but at the end of the day they collect the books and notebooks and the children go back to

the street. What is that? It is better to have a space for the children, where they stay, where they will not sniff glue as they do now, and where they can do their homework. (Ibtisam Aymen, August 2012, our translation)

In contrast, Amy Flynn's project works on vocational skills, with the objective of creating self-sustenance amongst the participants. A locally formed group was in charge of the project and decided on the exact content, as Amy explained:

There are literacy classes for the women; computer is more for the youth and in a way also for the women for their own computer. The courses on tailoring and crops are also for the women. But how they do it, the teaching, the materials and everything, I cannot tell. I do not know. (Amy Flynn, May 2011)

The three projects displayed different views on the role of education: education for peace, education to grow up in a safe environment, education to generate an income and independent living conditions. The projects and their founders seem to operate in quite isolated ways, running the risk of replicating history by creating 'islands of education', as Sommers (2005) called them (see also UNESCO 2011). The comment of a spokesman for the Ministry of General Education and Instruction is interesting in this respect:

Why do they not come and do the dirty work with us together? We would be very grateful. There are thousands out there. ... If they all came back, let us see what we can do together. ... We do not know what they are doing. We have been fighting over 20 years and they were over there, doing training. ... They have great ideas. ... They think everybody would be given a white collar job, but we have no money. (Director General Budgeting and Planning, Ministry of General Education and Instruction, personal communication, Juba, January 2013)

In the view of the government officer responsible for educational planning, members of the diaspora benefited from their time in exile and got trained, but they refused to come back now the conflict had finished or, if they were to come back they would do so with unrealistic ideas and demands.

These data indicate how views on the strategy for the reconstruction of education differ among the diaspora members and the Ministry of General Education and Instruction. Although they are operating in the same area with the same ultimate goal, there seems to be a lack of communication between them, which stands in the way of them becoming partners working for development. Below we discuss the necessity of rethinking partnerships to overcome this situation.

Rethinking partnerships

We started by creating a picture of youth who are travelling to their new country, probably filled with mixed feelings of hope and anxiety about the future in a country that is new to them. Most spectators will experience similar mixed feelings. Is the country ready to receive these newcomers? When she came back from visiting the project locations in northern Uganda and South Sudan, Amy wrote:

> I am not sure if I can survive in Uganda or South Sudan. To some extent, I now do understand why some of the people, especially the young ones, do what they are doing – drinking, marrying etc. – desperation and not knowing what to do, makes some of them turn to drinking as a coping mechanism. ... There is a big gap between the elderly and the youth, who are supposed to be the future leaders or heirs, in handling responsibilities and life style. I may be wrong, but I believe that these are some of the prices people pay due to the prolonged impact of wars, refuge, displacement etc. (Report on fieldtrip to South Sudan and northern Uganda, January 2012)

This observation illustrates the 'daunting' context discussed in the General Education Strategic Plan (MGEI 2012). Partnerships of all stakeholders involved are badly needed to provide basic services like education to the growing population of the new country. The diaspora are a group of promising partners (GoSS 2011; UNESCO 2011). Theories on capacity development and partnerships, which were originally developed to understand and improve North–South cooperation, stress the importance of contextualisation and ownership. This is where the members of the diaspora come in with their unique capabilities, which can be described by the concept of transnationalism. Our interest in studying the diaspora micro-development projects in education in South Sudan was to find out how this works in practice. Micro-development projects could be regarded as laboratories for new kinds of cooperation, which can inform partnerships on different levels. As De Haas and Rodriguez (2010) suggest, the study of the interaction between migration and development on the ground may contribute to the knowledge base on which effective partnerships for the reconstruction of education in South Sudan can be built.

The exploration of opportunities, challenges and perspectives on education concerning the micro-development projects led to three tentative conclusions regarding: (1) the position of the diaspora, (2) the receiving society, and (3) the interaction between the two. Firstly, the small-scale projects do not have a firm base in South Sudan yet. The only well-established project is in northern Uganda, where an active group on the ground is taking responsibility. In South Sudan, the diaspora have trouble finding partners with whom they can cooperate on an equal level. The projects run the risk of becoming isolated efforts without long-term effects, unacknowledged by the government, getting close to Deng's (2006) characterisation of the situation during wartime.

Secondly, the people leading the reconstruction of the educational sector profess in their policy papers that they need the diaspora, but also complain about their attitude, the lack of communication and commitments abroad which keep them from returning to their country. The hesitation about diaspora support is understandable from these experiences. Although further study of the receiving society remains to be done, we may already sense that the statements in the policy papers run the risk of only paying lip service to the potential of the diaspora. The result is that both sides seem to feel disappointed in the other and do not feel tempted to communicate.

Finally, there is so much to be done in reconstructing education: capacity development of teachers and other professionals, addressing educational needs of society, caring for war-affected groups and more. Discussion and dialogue are badly needed to identify common priorities. Meanwhile it seems there is hardly any communication between those who should work alongside each other to (re)build the educational sector in South Sudan.

Reviewing these three preliminary conclusions, one may say they reflect the 'old' way of thinking of two sides, the home and host country, the giving and receiving community. The concept of transnationalism would help to overcome this, referring to the effects of human mobility and pointing at the variegated people on both sides. At the same time, this concept seems to be of limited help in relation to capacity development and partnership building. It blurs differences, while the only way to build genuine partnerships is to discuss different backgrounds and experiences, especially in a post-conflict situation. Social learning and interactive knowledge production (Zeelen and Van der Linden 2009) are as indispensable in South–South partnerships as they are in North–South partnerships. Without these quality standards, partnerships run the risk of reproducing the same mistakes as in North–South cooperation, where one side is supposed to develop the other without leaving its comfortable base. Deng (2006) even speaks of 'paternalism' in this respect. Broadening the horizon, participating in international forums and studying lessons learned in other parts of Africa (see for example, Zeelen et al. 2010) may help to avoid a standoff and initiate a dialogue.

The challenge of being involved from a distance

Finally, we would like to question our own research question, which reflects an optimism that is also found in the literature on human mobility, development and transnationalism (UNDP 2009b). This is to be appreciated as it counterbalances the negative tone of publications on multiculturalism, but it should not conceal the human side of combining different worlds in one person. Throughout our research, we observed that, in spite of their rich resources, the activities of the diaspora do not necessarily flourish as one would expect them to. Although they are supposed to be able to implement capacity development in an endogenous way suiting the culture and traditions of the people on the ground, in-depth interviews give an insight into the challenge to experience transnationalism as a person.

The ideas of human mobility and transnationalism as a force for development should not be discarded, but should be complemented by studies on how migration and development interact on the ground. The resources and difficulties of the diaspora are reflections of what is happening in a changing world, where people move around, either by force or voluntarily. The personal involvement of the diaspora, which is undeniably present in each project, is a strength, but it can also be a weakness, leading to efforts in isolation. Partnerships connecting people and strategies are needed to retain the strength. Similarly, the boatloads of young people moving from North to South in Sudan can be regarded as additions to the worries of the country or as a potential for rebuilding the country, once their capabilities are strengthened in an appropriate way.

Acknowledgements

The authors want to thank the interviewees from the South Sudanese diaspora for the openness with which they shared their experiences and reflections on their beloved country with us. Also, we thank Cootje Logger, Paul Wabike and Jacques Zeelen for their comments to fine-tune the direction and the analysis of the research.

Notes

1. The Early School Leaving in Africa (ESLA) project is a joint research project of scholars from Africa and the Netherlands, carrying out research on causes, prevention and intervention strategies of early school leaving, leading to scientific publications and recommendations for policies and practices.
2. Pseudonyms are used for the organisations as well as for their initiators.
3. Examples of events attended by one or more of the authors are: Sudanese-Dutch family day, September 2010, organised by a group of Sudanese and Dutch people; documentary *Hinterland* on South Sudan, November 2011 in International Documentary Festival of Amsterdam; seminar on perspectives for South Sudan, March 2012 by Dutch NGO; workshops on micro-development projects, in April and July 2012 by the Diaspora Forum for Development.

References

ADPC (African Diaspora Policy Centre). 2008. "Engaging African Diaspora in Europe as Strategic Agents for Development in Africa." Accessed September 2, 2011. http://www.diaspora-centre.org/Migration_Development/ExpertMeetings/Enhancing_Dialogue_between_A/Engaging_African_Diaspora_in

Angucia, M. 2010. *Broken Citizenship: Formerly Abducted Children and Their Social Reintegration in Northern Uganda*. Amsterdam: Rozenberg.

Baarda, D. B., M. P. M. De Goede, and J. Teunissen. 2009. *Basisboek Kwalitatief Onderzoek* [Handbook on Qualitative Research]. 2nd ed. Groningen/Houten: Noordhoff Uitgevers.

Bauböck, R., and T. Faist, eds. 2010. *Diaspora and Transnationalism*. Amsterdam: Amsterdam University Press.

Bieckmann, F. 2012. *Soedan* [Sudan]. Amsterdam: Balans.

Breidlid, A. 2005. "Education in the Sudan: The Privileging of an Islamic Discourse." *Compare* 35 (3): 247–263.

Breidlid, A. 2010. "Sudanese Images of the Other: Education and Conflict in Sudan." *Comparative Education Review* 54 (4): 555–579. doi:10.1086/653814.

Brinkerhoff, D. W. 2010. "Developing Capacity in Fragile States." *Public Administration and Development* 30 (1): 66–78. doi:10.1002/pad.v30:1.

Broere, K. 2012. "Beter Leven in Vrij Zuid-Soedan Blijkt Na Een Jaar Ijdele Belofte [Better Life in South Sudan Remains an Empty Promise after a Year]." *De Volkskrant*, May 19, 17.

Creswell, J. W. 2007. *Educational Research*. Upper Saddle River, NJ: Pearson.

De Haas, H. 2005. "International Migration, Remittances and Development: Myths and Facts." *Third World Quarterly* 26 (8): 1269–1284. doi:10.1080/01436590500336757.

De Haas, H. 2010. "The Internal Dynamics of Migration Processes: A Theoretical Inquiry." *Journal of Ethnic and Migration Studies* 36 (10): 1587–1617. doi:10.1080/1369183X.2010.489361.

De Haas, H., and F. Rodriguez. 2010. "Mobility and Human Development." *Journal of Human Development and Capabilities* 11 (2): 177–184. doi:10.1080/19452821003696798.

Deng, L. B. 2006. "Education in Southern Sudan: War, Status, and Challenges of Achieving Education for All Goals." *Respect, Sudanese Journal for Human Rights' Culture and Issues of Cultural Diversity* 4: 1–27.

DRCMGP (Development Research Centre on Migration Globalisation and Poverty). 2009. "Diaspora and Development: Building Transnational Partnerships." Accessed September 2, 2011. http://www.migrationdrc. org/publications/briefing_papers/BP19.pdf

Eggers, D. 2006. *What is the What?* San Francisco, CA: McSweeney's.

Faist, T. 2010. "Towards Transnational Studies: World Theories, Transnationalisation and Changing Institutions." *Journal of Ethnic and Migration Studies* 36 (10): 1665–1687. doi:10.1080/1369183X.2010.489365.

Farag, A. I. 2012. "The Role of Adult Continuing Education in Providing Equitable Education Opportunities for the Pastoral Hawazma People in Selected Areas of Kordofan, Sudan." Paper presented at BAICE Conference, Cambridge, September 8–10.

Flick, U. 2006. *An Introduction to Qualitative Research*. 3rd ed. London: Sage.

GoSS (Government of South Sudan). 2005. *The Interim Constitution of Southern Sudan*. Juba: GoSS.

GoSS (Government of South Sudan). 2011. *South Sudan Development Plan 2011–2013. Realising Freedom, Equality, Justice, Peace and Prosperity for All*. Juba: GoSS.

Guo, S. 2013. *Transnational Migration and Lifelong Learning*. London/New York: Routledge.

Hennink, M., I. Hutter, and A. Bailey. 2010. *Qualitative Research Methods*. Los Angeles, CA: Sage.

Ibrahim, H. A. 2008. *Sudan: A Nation in Turmoil – is Education to Blame? An Analysis of Basic School Curriculums*. Saarbrücken: VDM Verlag.

Ionescu, D. 2006. *Engaging Diasporas as Development Partners for Home and Destination Countries: Challenges for Policy Makers*. Geneva: IOM.

Kiir Mayardit, S. 2011. Speech by the President of Republic of South Sudan, Salva Kiir Mayardit, at the closing ceremony of the International Engagement Conference, Washington, DC, December 15. Accessed March 15, 2013. http://www.thenewnation.net/special-report/55-special-report/265-president-kiirs-speech-at-the-closing-of-iec-in-washington-dc.html

Kleist, N. 2008a. "In the Name of Diaspora: Between Struggles for Recognition and Political Aspirations." *Journal of Ethnic and Migration Studies* 34 (7): 1127–1143. doi:10.1080/13691830802230448.

Kleist, N. 2008b. "Mobilising 'the Diaspora': Somali Transnational Political Engagement." *Journal of Ethnic and Migration Studies* 34 (2): 307–323. doi:10.1080/13691830701823855.

Lako, C. L., J. Van der Linden, and W. Deng. 2010. "South Sudan Inclusive: Education in a War-Torn Area." In *The Burden of Educational Exclusion*, edited by J. Zeelen, J. Van der Linden, D. Nampota, and M. Ngabirano, 141–155. Rotterdam/Taipei: Sense Publishers.

Ministry of General Education and Instruction (MGEI). 2012. *General Education Strategic Plan 2012–2017. Promoting Learning for All*. Draft. Juba: Ministry of General Education and Instruction.

Mohamoud, A. A. 2006. "African Diaspora and Post-Conflict Reconstruction in Africa." Accessed September 2, 2011. http://www.diis.dk/sw20382.asp

NBS (National Bureau of Statistics). 2012. *National Baseline Household Survey 2009 Report*. Juba: NBS.

Newland, K. 2004. *Beyond Remittances: The Role of Diaspora in Poverty Reduction in Their Countries of Origin*. Washington, DC: Migration Policy Institute.

NGO Forum Southern Sudan. 2009. "NGO Perspectives and Recommendations on Pooled Funding Mechanisms in Southern Sudan." Accessed March 15, 2013. http://southsudanngoforum.org/wp-content/uploads/2012/01/NGO%20Pooled%20Funding%20Paper.pdf

Njoka, J. M. 2007. "Diaspora Coordination Forum. Tapping into the Potential of the Southern Sudanese Diaspora (Workshop Report)." Accessed September 2, 2011. http://www.cmi.no/sudan/resources.cfm?id=779.

Nussbaum, M. C. 2011. *Creating Capabilities*. Cambridge, MA: The Belknap Press of Harvard University Press. doi:10.4159/harvard.9780674061200.

Obamba, M. O. 2013. "Transnational Knowledge Partnerships: New Calculus and Politics in Africa's Development." *Compare* 43 (1): 124–145.

OECD (Organisation for Economic Co-operation and Development). 2006. *The Challenge of Capacity Development*. Paris: OECD.

OECD (Organisation for Economic Co-operation and Development). 2010. *The Contribution of Diaspora Return to Post-Conflict and Fragile Countries*. Paris: OECD.

Oucho, J. O. 2009. "The African Diaspora and Home-Land Post-Conflict Reconstruction in Sub-Saharan Africa." Accessed September 2, 2011. www2.warwick.ac.uk/fac/soc/crer/events/african/ confp_john_oucho.doc

Sen, A. 1999. *Development as Freedom*. Oxford: Oxford University Press.

Sinatti, G. 2012. "From Global Migration to Local Development: Reflections on Diaspora Engagement for Effective Development." *Development Issues* 14 (1): 15–17.

Sommers, M. 2005. *Islands of Education: Schooling, Civil War and the Southern Sudanese (1983–2004)*. Paris: UNESCO/IIEP.

UNDP (United Nations Development Programme). 2009a. *Capacity Development: A UNDP Primer*. New York: UNDP.

UNDP. 2009b. *Overcoming Barriers: Human Mobility and Development*. New York: UNDP.

UNESCO (United Nations Educational, Scientific and Cultural Organisation). 2011. *Building a Better Future: Education for an Independent South Sudan*. Education for All Global Monitoring Report. Paris: UNESCO.

UNESCO. 2012. *Youth and Skills. Putting Education to Work*. EFA Global Monitoring Report 2012. Paris: UNESCO.

USAID. 2009a. "Feasibility Study for a Second-Phase Southern Sudanese Diaspora Program." Accessed September 2, 2011. http://www.cbtf-southernsudan.org/resource/507

USAID. 2009b. "Government of Southern Sudan Functional Capacity Prioritization Study." Accessed September 2, 2011. http://pdf.usaid.gov/pdf_docs/PNAD-U300.pdf

USAID. 2009c. "Human and Institutional Capacity Development (HICD) Policy Paper." Accessed September 2, 2011. http://www.usaid.gov/policy/ads/200/201maf.pdf

USAID. 2010. "Government of Southern Sudan Strategic Capacity Building Study." Accessed September 2, 2011. http://www.afdb.org/fileadmin/uploads/afdb/Documents/Policy-Documents/Capacity%20Building%20Assessment%2020%20July%20final.pdf

Van Beurden, J. 2006. *Sudan*. Amsterdam: KIT Publishers.

Van Naerssen, T., J. Kusters, and J. Schapendonk. 2006. *Afrikaanse Migrantenorganisaties in Nederland* [African Migrant Organisations in the Netherlands]. Nijmegen: Migration and Development Research Group.

Vertovec, S. 2009. "Towards Post-Multiculturalism? Changing Communities, Conditions and Contexts of Diversity." *International Social Science Journal* 61 (199): 83–95.

Vertovec, S. 2010. *Transnationalism*. London/New York: Routledge.

Walzer, C., ed. 2008. *Out of Exile*. San Francisco, CA: McSweeney's.

Zeelen, J., and J. Van der Linden. 2009. "Capacity Building in Southern Africa: Experiences and Reflections: Towards Joint Knowledge Production and Social Change in International Knowledge Development Cooperation." *Compare* 39 (5): 615–628. doi:10.1080/03057920903125644.

Zeelen, J., J. Van der Linden, D. Nampota, and M. Ngabirano, eds. 2010. *The Burden of Educational Exclusion*. Rotterdam/Taipei: Sense Publishers.

Negotiating differences: cosmopolitan experiences of international doctoral students

Başak Bilecen

Faculty of Sociology, Bielefeld University, Bielefeld, Germany

Drawing on the literature on international student experiences and identities, this study discusses theories of identity from a social constructionist perspective. 'Identification' is the preferred term to describe a dynamic process through which students negotiate the meaning of their identities in different societies and communities. Based on interviews with 35 international doctoral students from two graduate schools in Germany, the article illustrates the significance of international mobility for education when external 'differences' are appreciated and contribute to cosmopolitan imaginations and when internal differences are created in relation to 'Others' in the host society. The article contributes to the literature on international student mobility by providing a fine-grained analysis of student identification, showing how the discourse of difference is used as a double strategy.

Introduction

The increasing presence of international students on campuses worldwide is becoming the norm rather than an exception. For instance, according to the latest OECD (2012) report, 'the number of foreign students increased from 2.1 to 4.1 million, an increase of 99%. Consequently, the share of tertiary students who are foreign students grew by more than 10% between 2000 and 2010' (362) due to the globalisation and internationalisation of higher education systems. While the structure of higher education institutions is transforming into what could be called corporate machines, with students as their customers and the corporations as their clients, this globalised knowledge economy has led to spatial disparities and has caused the universities to recruit an increasing number of international students under the banner of internationalisation (Bolsmann and Miller 2008; Stromquist and Monkman

2000). International students play a crucial role in these processes, and the policies to recruit them extend beyond the economic sphere to include political, social and cultural elements (Brooks and Waters 2011). However, the ever-increasing number of international students has attracted the interest of academics, universities and policy makers because they are also attributed and studied as belonging to a highly skilled and mobile demographic. Although Germany has a long tradition of international students attending its institutions of higher education, recruiting such students has become a major issue over the past few decades, particularly since the introduction of new measures designed to promote the Europeanisation and internationalisation of institutions of higher education.

There have been several lines of research on international student mobility in various disciplines, ranging from research on intercultural communication and adaptation (e.g. Gill 2007; Gu, Schweisfurth, and Day 2010; Murphy-Lejeune 2002a, 2002b), to social support through friendship networks (Bilecen 2012; Bochner, McLeod, and Lin 1977; Furnham and Alibhai 1985), to cross-cultural study experiences (Brown 2009; Hellstén and Prescott 2004; Montgomery 2010; Robinson-Pant 2005, 2009). There are also a group of studies from various disciplines that have focused on the identities of international students (e.g. Ghosh and Wang 2003; King and Ruiz-Gelices 2003; Koehne 2005, 2006; Rizvi 2000, 2005; Schmitt, Spears, and Branscombe 2002; Singh, Rizvi, and Shrestha 2007; Torres, Jones, and Renn 2009; van Mol 2011). However, studies on this type of mobility are rather few and far between, and none of them has addressed the central question of how international students' identifications are negotiated in relation to various other types of 'Others'.

Although much excellent work has been done on issues such as the effects of studying abroad on cosmopolitan identity, scholars investigating the identities of international students have not fully explored the importance of 'the Other' as a set of reference points that play a part in creating, differentiating and sustaining these identities. But without a comprehensive understanding of such issues, we are left with only an inadequate analysis of identities and identifications. This study uses the term 'identification' rather than 'identity' to dispense with solid semantic implications of 'identity', thus emphasising its dynamic, relational and process nature. In doing so, this article fills this gap in the literature by examining how identifications are negotiated in relation to 'the Other' to more fully elucidate the hitherto unexplored relationship between the multiplicity of 'the Other' and the ways in which 'difference' is used as a double strategy.

Another point worth noting is that the literature generally focuses on undergraduate students because the years before graduation are believed to be critical in shaping students' attitudes towards learning and their perceptions of it (Hayden and Thompson 1995; Trotter and Roberts 2006). Almost no research has been done on the experiences of graduates and postgraduates (exceptions include Bilecen 2012; Rizvi 2010; Robertson 2011) and most of the studies that focus on these groups do not actually distinguish between them (some examples include Hsieh 2006; Lee and Rice 2007; Tian and Lowe 2009). However, postgraduate students are a very important subject of study because they are in a phase of transition from being consumers of education to producers who are appreciated for their academic achievements and innovation capabilities, which will have an influence on the reputation of the university and, later, of the country. More-over, their status is also seen differently depending on the educational con-text and on whether they are students, postgraduate students or researchers. In general, the motivations of these individuals are 'self-reflexive and not driven by the preferences of parents' (Rizvi 2010, 163), due to several fac-tors such as age, class, familial obligations and financial circumstances, to name just a few.

This article begins with a discussion of discourses of identification in the literature on student experiences and other relevant theoretical lenses. It then proceeds to describe the methodology and the sample of the study. Next, based on the empirical evidence, it illustrates the narratives of international doctoral students and examines how 'difference' is referred to in their narra-tives both as appreciation and as a leverage point. The concluding section discusses the contributions of the study.

Student identifications in transnational graduate education

Due to the increased presence of international students and faculty mem-bers, cultural differences now exist in all contemporary educational settings. Such diversity is found in both international and transnational settings. Graduate education today is not only internationalised – in the sense that it incorporates all aspects of higher education systems or institutions (Thorsby 1991) – but is transnationalised as well. Scholars who take a transnational perspective position are mobile subjectivities within social spaces that con-nect various national territories, rather than imagining them moving back and forth between two restricted states in a dichotomous manner and the exchange of one national identity for another. Thomas Faist (2000) clearly defines 'transnational social spaces' as, 'combinations of ties and their con-tents, positions in networks and organisations and networks of organisations that can be found in at least two geographically and internationally distinct places' (197). In this sense, transnational social spaces provide contexts for interaction and transaction as well as for the organisation, construction and reconstruction of identifications, social networks, flows of ideas, knowledge, goods and practices. Present-day graduate education thus has a transnational character, in that it connects various different contexts of education, each of which affects students, faculty members, administrative staff, institutions and nation-states. 'Analysing the mobility of international doctoral students by a transnational lens suggests the idea that they are in fact living in oscillating worlds at the crossroads of the economic, political, social, personal and academic contexts of different nation-states' (Bilecen 2009, 10). There is also a 'spatial diversity' in international higher education that creates inequalities, and different educational places are closely interlinked. As a result, the higher education space is 'relational', making it necessary to explore the various social, cultural and political meanings of student mobility (Brooks and Waters 2011).

There has been growing academic interest in studying the identities of international students, who are, without any doubt, mobile subjectivities, embedded in transnational social spaces and involved in cross-border activities and practices. Scholars working in this area have referred to their identities as 'hyphenated' (Ghosh and Wang 2003), 'transnational' (Ghosh and Wang 2003), 'hybrid' (Koehne 2005, 2006), 'European' (King and Ruiz-Gelices 2003; Van Mol 2011) and 'cosmopolitan' (Rizvi 2005; Singh, Rizvi, and Shrestha 2007). All of these scholars have also considered how international students perceive and present themselves, rather than taking essentialising approaches by studying international students as a homogenous group. For instance, Fazal Rizvi (2005) has argued that international education perpetuates a strategic cosmopolitan imaginary identity that is more of an instrumentalist perspective than a moral one, leading to cosmopolitan solidarity. He has also suggested that the identities of international doctoral students continue to be involved in national and global discourses of power and class, systems of history and social interactions, all of which are embedded in transnational social spaces that fabricate the students' being, belonging and becoming (Rizvi 2010).

The studies of Norma Koehne provide a similar post-modern and post-structuralist analysis to investigate identity constructions and the internal and external subjective positionings of international students. She notes that international students cannot simply be characterised as 'the Other' in a binary opposition to local students. Rather, they must be meticulously examined in their own right as agents who not only reproduce their own multiple subjectivities, but also question the discursive positionings assigned to them by others (Koehne 2005, 2006).

Another study in this area is by Ghosh and Wang (2003), who take a different methodological perspective, utilising self-reflexive narratives derived from their own experiences as international students in Canada to analyse transnationalism and identity creation. At this point, it is important to truly understand the meaning and usage of 'identity'. The following is Richard Jenkins' (2008) definition of the term, which he distinguishes from 'identification', although the two terms are quite often used interchangeably:

[I]dentity is the human capacity – rooted in language – to know 'who's who' (and hence 'what's what'). This involves knowing who we are, knowing who others are, them knowing who we are, us knowing who they think we are, and so on: a multi-dimensional classification or mapping of the human world and our places in it, as individuals and as members of collectivities .... It is a process – *identification* – not a 'thing'. It is not something that one can *have*, or not; it is something that one *does*. (5, emphasis in original)

In the same vein, Jenkins (2008) also argues that social identities are produced as a result of the individuals' understanding of their own selves, their social interactions and their sense of similarity and difference to others. In other words, social identities are socially constructed through negotiating the dialectic of similarity and difference every individual has in relation to others. If identities are relational, it is plausible to state that there can be no 'us' without 'them' and that difference is generated through relations (Merton 1968). Socially constructed identities involve a reflexive process, which underlies the agency of individuals as well as power in a given negotiated relation. Therefore, the representation and content of social identities are influenced by social discourses and political ideologies (Callero 2003).

However, the concept of identity is essentialist and has unifying and reifying connotations, which makes it analytically sterile (de Federico de la Rúa 2007). This article agrees with the ideas of de Federico de la Rúa (2007) and Brubaker and Cooper (2000), who note that the concept of 'identification' should be used instead of 'identity' because it is emancipated from solid semantic implications. 'Identification', as used in this article, thus refers to the dynamic process through which students negotiate the meaning of their identities in different societies and communities.

Because this article takes a social constructionist perspective (see Burr 1995), 'identification' does not refer to a fixed and unified concept of 'being' in the sense of a given or a product bound to only one cultural frame of reference and meaning, envisaging shared norms, traditions and values. Rather, it is understood to be one of articulation (Hall 1996) between the social actor and the identity positions or resources placed at their disposal. In other words, it is a social enactment 'in continuous play with history, culture and power' (Hall 1990, 225). 'Identification' is based on social relations. It is an ongoing process of constructing an individual sense of self by choosing with which individuals, with which groups and with what to associate oneself. It is composed of relational belongings or affiliations with groups or categories in which its fluidity is embedded, rather than static entities. Identification thus involves active meaning-making processes of the self through social interactions that are influenced by the dynamics of international mobility for the purpose of education.

The identities of international students, 'are clearly shaped not only by their personal histories, cultural traditions and professional aspirations but are also continually reshaped by new cultural experiences, but in ways that are neither uniform nor predictable' (Rizvi 2005, 4). The question is, what role does international education play as students negotiate fluid identifications and challenge the essentialist cultural perspectives.

'[T]o exist is to be called into being in relation to an Otherness' (Bhabha 1994b, 117). This Otherness is constructed through stereotyping and articulating differences in discourses. Expressed differently, it is what is told about the Other that is used to construe the Other. Homi Bhabha (1994a) further argues that a group is made the Other so it can be controlled by the powerful, but that it is not possible to know another group to the fullest, so their idea of what the Other is or how it is constructed is always incomplete. However, the Other has always been positioned in binary opposition to the Self – the coloniser and the colonised – or, in this specific case, international students and host students. However, international students can construct other groups as the Other to define themselves as occupying a different position in society.

The main argument of the following sections is that identification is inspired by cross-cultural interactions and cosmopolitan repertoires and used as a double strategy, assembled in appreciation of difference and self-differentiation through higher educational credentials. This article regards cosmopolitanism, 'as a particular worldview characterized by the capacity to mediate between different cultures' (Mau, Mewes, and Zimmermann 2008, 2), as a state of mind, a manner of conscious open-mindedness to the world and to other cultures (Hannerz 1990, 1996; Vertovec and Cohen 2002).

Methodology

Extensive semi-structured interviews with international doctoral students (21 female and 14 male) from two universities in Germany provide the empirical basis of this study.[1] With 20 different nationalities, the interviews cover a wide range of ethnic and religious backgrounds.[2] The interviewees were between 25 and 41 years old, and all of them had had previous international experience, including participating in exchange programmes, working as interns in international organisations, attending language courses or working and studying abroad, at some point in their lives.

The participants were chosen from among the students of two graduate schools in two different cities, both of which receive funding under the 'Excellence Initiative' programme.[3] The students enrolled in the two institutions were chosen for two reasons.

The first was to avoid methodological nationalism, that is, studying global phenomena from a territorialist geographical perspective (Basch, Glick-Schiller, and Szanton-Blanc 1994), as has been done in the literature on migration and international education. The focus of this study is not on ethnic or national communities as units of analysis (see Glick-Schiller, Caglar, and Guldbrandsen 2006; Glick-Schiller, Darieva, and Gruner-Domic 2011). Rather than treating international students who live their transnational lives as a homogeneous group, it uses a transnational lens for sampling to include students from various countries and cultures and to examine the differences between them.

The second reason is that the aim of this article is to examine students who study at non-English-speaking universities in non-English-speaking countries. Previous studies have almost exclusively considered the experiences of international students at English-speaking universities, and few, if any, studies have been conducted focusing on international students at non-English-speaking universities who are affected by processes of internationalisation. Germany is a popular country among students. It is one of the highest-ranking non-English-speaking countries in the world and attracts international students from many diverse backgrounds. The fact that Germany is also in the process of internationalisation and Europeanisation makes it a very interesting case study. The main tool used for data analysis is qualitative content analysis (Mayring 2000), 'a research method for the subjective interpretation of the content of the text data through the systematic classification process of coding and identifying themes or patterns' (Hsieh and Shannon 2005, 1278). Qualitative content analysis is used to examine latent meanings, themes and patterns in transcribed interviews, and the interviewees' statements are treated as social constructions rather than facts. It should be noted that, of course, this study is only a snapshot of the interviewees' identification of who they were at a particular point in time and space, so it does not necessarily say anything about their essential selves.

Enjoying the difference

When the students talked about their experience studying abroad they frequently used the word 'different', as in different culture, different people, different lifestyle, different working environment, different language, different academic culture and so on. Their transnational experience also involved seeing different places and cultures, meeting different people, working with different colleagues, seeing different ways of living, tasting different cuisines and consuming things that were different from what they knew. The content of difference can be very diverse and may include geographical and tangible aspects, traditions, customs and daily life practices and the attitudes and perspectives of people. The participants were not directly asked what they thought it was that was different. Rather, their narratives always included comparisons, and they pointed out both positive and negative differences. National difference was basically taken for granted. For example, one recurrent theme in the narratives was that 'this is the German way', which shows how nationality is attributed as a 'divisive' factor to delineate societal and cultural boundaries. Other examples from the interviews include: 'Germans just say what they think', 'they are much colder and much more concerned with themselves and their personal success' and 'they have everything very well-organised'.

However, this discursive and objectified difference is achieved by essentialising stereotypes to some degree, especially stereotypes of the host society – 'It is to imply an internal sameness and external difference or otherness' (Werbner 1997, 228). In a sense, the negotiation of identification is a process of essentialising or stereotyping 'us' and 'them', so the negotiation of difference or sameness is a crucial aspect of generating 'differently centred worlds' (Clifford 1997, 27). However, 'the German way' is also appreciated because it provides favourable contexts of education and research, as these examples illustrate:

> In Germany, you can criticise your professor. In a seminar, you can simply say, 'I totally disagree with you.' You can say that. But you cannot say that in East Asia. (Huang[4], 34)[5]

> I think if one manages to complete a successful PhD in Germany it would be very good for his career in any other field, in Europe. Germans are known as people who don't just let go of things. They look carefully through everything they are entitled to and I think this is very good and if I learn that my work is valued here that I know for myself that what I do is right because nobody would just give it to me because of this or that. It would only be because of what I've done and because I've deserved it. (Mihai, 25)

> Even before I came to Germany, I already knew its quality in education .... Germany enjoys a good reputation in education and also in PhD education. (Ji, 28)

The interviewees also appreciated the way of life in their country of education and adopted typical daily routines in their everyday lives rather than just consuming:

> For example, the garbage, it is not divided in Russia there is not this distinction between the different types of garbage. Then I see for example [in Russia] a basket where you have your *Müll* (trash), plastic and glass, everything together and that's disturbing me now. (Irina, 27)

> I mean that simply living in Germany, in Europe, is fine, you know. It's much better ... this kind of spillover. If you enjoy your life in general you also enjoy your job more. So, the general appreciation of quality of life you have, kind of spills over into other domains, in job as well. So yes, living is simply better. (Natalia, 33)

Although the content of difference appears to be ambiguous, the perception of its existence in various settings (in relation not only to the home and host countries but also to other places) was a fundamental and quite remarkable element of the narratives, and being confronted with the difference has made their experience unique and has caused them to develop various ways of identification. These identifications were constantly constructed, reconstructed and negotiated as the interviewees gained new international and educational experience and adopted new positions. When asked about studying in other countries, and specifically in Germany, the interviewees gave answers which included aspects such as 'seeing differ-ences', 'learning to cope with the different', 'adapting to the difference', 'enjoying meeting with different people', 'different contacts', 'different views on the world', 'meeting people from different countries', 'exploring different cities', 'working in a different environment' and 'my life here is different'.

All of the interviewees talked mostly about their positive learning experi-ences in Germany, how they benefited from their studies and how they appreciated being educated in a different way because they were 'learning to interact with a whole different' (Dulani, 28). This is how Saskia put it:

> I think living abroad definitely it's a cliché, but it does broaden your horizon. [laughs] It gives you a different perspective, and you learn a lot just having a different environment and a different focus. (Saskia, 25)

The interviewees clearly perceived and were aware of differences, and they appreciated them because they become more open-minded to the existing differences. It is equally important to note that the differences used as points of reference for self-identification were not used in the form of binary cate-gories, meaning that the interviewees talked not only about differences between Germany and their countries of origin, but also of differences they had learned about from cross-cultural encounters with other international students and from prior international educational experiences. Difference is something to be seen and enjoyed – such as new tastes – as the following example shows:

> I learned here different cuisines, good wine, because in Russia wine is really expensive and Russian wine doesn't taste so good … here one can buy differ-ent types of wine at the supermarkets such as Italian and Spanish, and enjoy them, and it certainly isn't very expensive. Or take food, for example: mussels are very expensive in Russia. (Natasha, 31)

Seeing and enjoying differences goes hand in hand with seeing new places, cities and countries. The interviewees appreciated being in the middle of Europe, being able to visit various countries and simply observ-ing and enjoying what is happening in the city. This appreciative narrative became clear when the interviewees were asked what they did in their city, what their daily routines involved and how and why they enjoyed being in Germany. This is how Mihai from Macedonia, who studied in Italy and is now studying in Germany and working in Belgium, sees his situation:

I have been in Italy, I lived in Italy, and I have travelled almost everywhere in Europe .... I enjoy travelling. I like to observe different types of people, different ways of life, I enjoy seeing and living those different things out there .... Sometimes it is not easy to commute between my work and my studies, but I manage it because I enjoy it. (Mihai, 25)

These examples clearly show that there was an emphasis on the difference of 'the Other', 'German society' or 'the German culture', rather than on the fact that the interviewees were different themselves. They referred to their connection to a new place and to the local way of life. In Saskia's case, for instance, separating garbage has been internalised and has been incorporated into her lifestyle in Germany. This means that it is not only about staying out of the context and consuming, rather, the interviewees also interacted and incorporated the local way of life into their own, a behaviour that is indicative of cosmopolitanism as defined by Ulf Hannerz (1990), who describes cosmopolitanism as the willingness and capability to engage with the cultural other through face-to-face interactions experienced in the 'round of everyday life in a community' (240). The interviewees saw, enjoyed and learned from differences they encountered and social interactions made them have a more tolerant outlook and become cosmopolitan. In other words, consumption is the primary way of enjoying the differences of new places, be it by enjoying a variety of foods, venues, cafés and restaurants or by being educated in a prestigious yet different system. It becomes clear from the narratives that international doctoral students praise and enjoy differ-ence, which is one of the major principles of cosmopolitanism and the pro-cess of identifying oneself as cosmopolitan.

To sum up, the interviewees very much enjoyed and appreciated the dif-ferences. With their previous and current international relational experiences, they are able to spot and evaluate what difference is. Difference is embed-ded in relationality – to be able to think about difference(s), at least two entities are needed, as is interaction between them. The Other acts as the necessary premise for negotiating and constructing self-identification. While this section has focused more closely on the difference of the multiple Oth-ers involved, the next section will discuss cases in which the interviewees emphasised how they themselves are different.

Difference as a leverage point – 'I am not like all these migrants'

There are a number of external factors leading international doctoral students to identify themselves with certain categories, such as belonging to a certain nationality or region, or being a part of an international student group, or identifying themselves as academic researchers. The main external factor is constructing 'otherness' from the perspective of the majority soci-ety. Being made foreigners at various levels (legal status, educational and academic background) may cause international students to get more attached to and to identify with their own culture. For instance, research on Asian international students often works with generalisations, describing them as uncritical, passive, obedient, lacking analytical and argumentative abilities and even incapable, due to the fact that they are 'Asian' (Samuelowicz 1987). One of the 'Asian' doctoral students (Ji, 28) talked about how he was trying to 'cope with the new conditions and manage the cultural differences' when, based on the negative stereotype, he was made 'the Other' in the classroom and was identified based on cultural habits or nationality, the main category referred to in the interview:

> I had experienced that [deal with cultural differences] when I first come to Germany and have a seminar with the fellows, and I carry somehow the Chinese students' habits as I told, which means, the Chinese students do not criticise, do not behave so critical in the discussion. And he [my professor] once told me that 'this is a doctors' colloquium, you don't have to agree with them, you have to be critical and actually understand and defend all your points'.

This moment of questioning the differences during the present educational experience illustrates how identification results in the 'articulation of difference' (Bhabha 1994a, 3), with the relationality of identification occurring both externally and internally. The interviewee Ji was made 'the Other' by the faculty member based on his 'obedient' behaviour, which was perceived to be typical of 'Asian' students. However, Ji considered himself to be more 'flexible' in terms of spatial belonging and less flexible with regard to national aspects, in that he accepted his being different while noting the differences that others in the host society perceived:

> There's always a distance between me and them [the Germans], we can say, because I have not so much background of this culture, and they also realise I'm different from them. So I still feel there's a difference between each other.

Another interviewee told how domestic students made him 'the Other' by switching between languages depending on his absence or presence in class. Different languages are embedded in idiosyncratic cultural roots and, even though some languages have the same roots, over time they have all been developed and diversified in different countries and regions. Language represents certain cultural elements, changes in history, certain ways of living and developments in a country. To put it differently, language is not only a symbolic system but also a system to symbolise, which can be used to 'claim and reject identities, to signal relationships and to display memberships' (Liddicoat, Crozet, and Lo Bianco 1999, 50). When the international doctoral students interviewed for this study went to live in a multilingual environment that involved different living and working languages, they were also made 'the Other' based on language, a point that has been largely neglected in the literature:

> Out of 15 students, I was the only *foreign*. And within this colloquium we have weekly, out of 30 or 40 people I was the only *foreign student* and I was the only one who was not German speaker. So while the colloquium was conducted in English, I felt it was just because of me, you know? And anytime I would have been late I'll enter the room and I realized and *they speak German,* and when I enter they immediately switch in *English.* (Damjan, 33)

While the interviewees were made 'the Other', at the same time, they identified themselves as different from other reference groups in society, namely the groups of immigrants who were already living in the country. According to social identity theory, individuals pursue membership in groups that grant them a positive social identity (Tajfel and Turner 1979) and that are inclined to preserve positive distinctiveness through inter-group comparisons. Unfavourable comparisons with out-groups confer low status, while favourable comparisons with out-groups give the in-group a high status. Thus, in order to achieve a positive social identity, individuals are prompted to identify with high-status groups rather than with low-status groups. A number of studies (e.g., Furnham and Bochner 1986; Lalonde, Taylor, and Moghaddam 1992) have found that groups of immigrants and refugees commonly identify themselves with, or are identified as, 'Others', which has certain negative connotations such as 'foreigner', 'alien' or what Bhabha (1994a) has called 'the colonised'. When inter-group social comparisons are made in a new setting, these groups are usually accorded a low status, whereas international doctoral students perceive themselves to be legitimately high in status and class because of their high level of education, leading to a positive distinctiveness from comparison groups – in this case, immigrant groups from their country of origin. In other words, they redefine what they want to be identified with and, 'minimize the ethnic aspect of their social (ethnic) identity by projecting their personal and situational identity instead [they] often foreground their current role and the status it brings, in an attempt to convince the others that it is the here and now that matters' (Valenta 2009, 359). The interviewees showed a general tendency to disassociate themselves from groups of immigrants of the same nationality already living in Germany. From a sociological point of view, social class is a crucial determinant of group identification and of specific cultural patterns of consumption, behaviour and lifestyle (Bourdieu 1984; Lamont 1992). Individuals who are more or less in the same social class have similar lifestyles and deal with similar realities (Tomlinson 2003). They may also have similar interests and predispositions. These similarities would make it comfortable for them to socialise with each other, to identify with their own group and to dissociate themselves from other groups of immigrants already living in Germany.

Due to their higher educational levels and their different lifestyles, international doctoral students considered their cosmopolitan orientations and values in many instances as incompatible with those of other immigrant groups. As a result, the interviewees were not particularly interested in developing relationships with those groups unless they are in need. On the contrary, they preferred to distance themselves from these groups by making references to their being different because of their own educational achievements. The interviewees also implied that not having relationships or not identifying with other groups was a question of status or class, with answers usually containing phrases such as 'they are immigrants', 'they are workers', 'they came here earlier to work', 'they are not skilled', 'they are not educated', 'they are old', 'we don't have anything in common', 'they are different', 'I am here to study', 'I am writing my thesis, I have no time for such contacts', 'it depends on how they came to Germany', 'they have completely different backgrounds', 'I don't want [to get involved socially with them]', 'they are concentrated on their families' and 'I am not part of them'.

The interviewees were also asked to describe their relationships to those who belonged to the same ethnicity or nationality or with whom they speak the same native language.[6] They always depicted their relations with their other international friends who were from the same country or were native speakers of the same language. They only reflected on their experiences when they were asked specifically about their relationships to established groups of migrants already living in Germany. However, the co-national, co-ethnic or co-language relationships were very much limited to the circle of friends from university regardless of year or degree:

> I have *a lot* of Chinese friends here because, you know, for Chinese people, they like to gather together, to have dinner or to have fun. And there is also the Chinese students association. I think, maybe in every city in Germany. It is Chinese tradition, that we visit each other often. (Dao-ming, 27)

When asked about her involvement with Chinese immigrant groups, she stated:

> I think there are only a *few* Chinese people immigrating to Germany, and so far I didn't know any of *them.*

Another interviewee stated that her relationships with the wider Russian-speaking community in Germany were limited to the academic world, except when she needed support in finding a dentist with whom she believed she could communicate more easily because she needed the comfort of her native language during the medical treatment. Her example also illustrates how some interviewees 'homogenise' migrant groups as 'the wider Russian community' or 'the Russian-speaking PhD students':

I have no idea. I, um, I only know those Russian-speaking people who also do their PhD in our graduate school coming from different countries. I think these are the only Russian-speaking people I'm in contact with. ... As for outer Russian-speaking community so far, I didn't even have *the idea of contacting* other Russian people. I have no connection and I never *even had an idea* of finding a connection. I can tell you a friend of mine, from St. Petersburg she has a friend in Hamburg and I met this friend once because I had a present to transmit, so that's how we met and exchanged our contact and now I will contact her because I need to find a dentist and I'd like to find a Russian-speaking dentist. (Natalia, 33)

This shows that in most cases the interviewees received assistance from the wider immigrant communities who had the practical information or contacts the interviewees needed. Nationality was often negotiated flexibly, meaning that national ties were activated when practical assistance was needed. However, this did not necessarily lead to close interaction. One reason may be that the interviewees were 'supposed to be' those with the higher status and the higher level of education, 'those who control mobility' (Brooks and Waters 2011). But, at the same time, they were being made 'the Other' by the majority society or by their academic environment, through language switching or cultural stereotyping. As a result, these individuals may find it difficult to admit that the migrants from the 'lower' social strata in the country of origin 'who are controlled by mobility' (Brooks and Waters 2011) are now in 'more' powerful positions due to their knowledge of German language or the healthcare system. Another example is Teresa, who knew some people in the Mexican immigrant community in Germany. Teresa identified with the general categorical membership they shared, but she had no close relationships with this community, nor did she share any interpersonal context with it because she thought that friendship cannot be based on nationality alone but must also be based on common interests:

If you get to know people there is obviously a link between these Mexicans and myself. We make reference to the same culture, we miss sort of the same things, and so on. But when you exhaust these memories and these things, then you must find something in common with the other person. And if there's nothing, then it's hard to make friendship out of that and to me you cannot become friend with another person just because you come from the same country. (Teresa, 26)

For other interviewees, not socialising with those of the same nationality is a deliberate choice. Ligaya, for example, made it clear that during her previous and present international educational experiences she was more interested in getting involved with people from other cultures, rather than with people from cultures that were similar to her own:

> I don't mind being with them [immigrants from her country of origin] I don't feel ashamed being with them. I love being with them, it's just that I don't really feel the need to find that sense of community with Filipinos. When I was doing this course in the Netherlands, for example, I never got along well with Filipinos, but I didn't hang out with them often. Because for me it's such a waste that you know this is your chance to be exposed to another culture and other nationalities, and then if you want Filipinos you can always find them in the Philippines, you don't have to go to Germany to be with them. [laughs] So that's always been my attitude. I would go out with other nationalities rather than my own, but because I think it's just that's how I want it. (Ligaya, 35)

Irina further illustrated that although she had friends who were of the same nationality, they all belonged to the same academic environment. She stated that she did not need contact with immigrant groups because she did not share their interests and she preferred to experience other cultures instead, including German culture:

> I don't see it [to have contact with immigrants of her nationality] is somehow necessary, I have enough friends here both German-speaking and international friends from other countries. I know, let's say some groups, where for example they sing Russian song or something like this, a cultural event, many go there. Of course, I would know more Russian people if I go there but I don't feel ... that it lacks me, I can speak Russian, I do rather speak German here, I have enough friends also in Russia .... They came here 20 years ago or something like this, they have a completely different background and purpose. We don't have common interests. They are somehow people who are very concentrated on their family. (Irina, 27)

Social classes, or collectives of individuals who occupy similar positions in social spaces structured by power and resources, are actively produced by the interviewees through their everyday practices of sense-making (Bourdieu 1985). Different classes elucidate different lifestyles based on habits, which are related to education, occupation, access to capital and their inclination to differ from or conform to other social groupings. Symbolic practices, such as not singing a particular national song or choosing to speak other languages, define social groups and classes. This 'vision of divisions' brings the implicit social groups to the surface and into the light (Bourdieu 1985, 1989). Even if the interviewees form relationships with immigrant groups who share the same nationality, there is always a justification for doing so, such as indicating a higher status of the groups contacted. It also exemplifies how interviewees construct the immigrant community, which can have diversities within itself and does not necessarily have to be a homogeneous entity, unlike the cultural stereotypes perpetuated by mainstream society:

I met Veli's sister Leyla and her husband, a small group. I thought for a moment that all Turks here are like those people, but this issue is different. Of course, I knew that there are also normal, classical Turkish families as we know, but I thought that [this small circle] would have relations with the [Turkish immigrant families]. But that was not the case. I met the first Turkish community here … such radicals, a Turkish minority community within the Turkish community and *they are also* a different group. For instance, it was in a 'Turkish night', which means that when we get together we don't speak about normal things … you know, when two Turks come together, they say things like, 'Well, we are fine, how are you, and how are the kids?' In our case, everyone wants to talk about things like 'What is it like to be from the East? What does it mean to be Western? How European do you feel you are?' Or we choose a topic and everyone talks about it …. It is a very interesting group, very marginal, as far as I understand they shut themselves off from the Turkish community here and after I met them I also started to see their identity problems. (Ayşe, 27)

In the case of international PhD students, this kind of identification involves flexible external and internal processes. The host society, including the native students and professors, were the main external influence, in that they 'othered' the interviewees but also appreciated their being different. In addition, identification was influenced by an internal group dynamic. The interviewees developed a cosmopolitan imagination because they were appreciated as international students, belonged to that group, cherished the higher level of education and the higher status that came with it and disassociated themselves from migrants of the same nationality, ethnicity or language.

Concluding remarks

Identification is by no means a new process, but with the accelerated flows of individuals, cultures and ideas, the intensity, range and frequency of encounters with the culturally diverse are ever increasing in our postmodern world (Featherstone 1995). The culturally different act as reference points in shaping one's own identifications by using relational means. In other words, interacting and engaging with 'them' and their differences and their 'othernesses' are a way of defining 'us'. The reflexive and relational process of identification negotiation is mediated through contact with diversity. As these cases of international doctoral students have demonstrated, engaging with different 'Others' raises awareness of difference, which cannot only be enjoyed, but which is also a way of better perceiving the self as being 'different' as well. Individuals who cross borders for educational purposes encounter the different, have access to new resources and live the difference, which they can either accept or reject. When they were made 'the Other' by 'Others' whom they appreciated, the individuals interviewed for this study perceived themselves as being different from groups with whom they shared the same nationality, ethnicity, language and in some instances even the same class. This raises the question of why the stereotyping 'coloniser' language (Bhabha 1994b) could be effective for generations but has been challenged, considering that the examples illustrate that they are not always perceived as homogenous inferior 'Others'.

Koehne (2005) notes that many international students who encounter differences and multiple meaning systems in the host country negotiate their identifications in creative and synergised ways, by combining ideas, concepts and cultural products from their country of origin and other countries, and meaning systems from their current country of education in producing and reproducing their identification. As the narratives of the interviewees have shown, the main common reference point that underlies the differences between themselves and other status groups is clearly their education abroad with other international students: their symbolic property. While enjoying the difference refers to the international educational experiences of the international doctoral students, difference as a leverage point is associated with their higher educational achievements and, thus, their status and class. Common lifestyles and similar socialising and classification patterns illustrate that they form a social group with a higher status. Their symbolic property is their main discourse of identification, which could be regarded as cosmopolitan because the students emphasised their tolerance and openness, if only in relation to certain groups. Therefore, international doctoral students choose to occupy a position in social space that is characterised as transnational, not only through the relationality of higher education institutions but also through articulating everyday practices and thus developing cosmopolitan identifications.

This study makes a contribution to the literature on international student mobility by providing an empirical analysis that is more than a mere description of patterns of international student mobility, in that it examines identifications of such students to reveal the social and cultural meanings of their mobility, as suggested by Brooks and Waters (2011). By examining the strategies the interviewees used to construct differences, this study takes Rizvi's (2000, 2005, 2010) analyses of the cosmopolitan identities of international students one step further. In doing so, it takes a closer look at the various reference points of difference involved in negotiating identification and creating a cosmopolitan imagination. It also illustrates how the students experience cosmopolitanism and how the dynamics of discourses of difference are shaped. It shows how what is perceived as 'the different' is indeed heterogeneous and how similarities can be constructed as differences.

Acknowledgements

I would like to extend my gratitude to the Special Issue guest editors Madeleine Arnot and Claudia Schneider and the two anonymous referees of this paper, whose

117

comments were extremely helpful in revising the original draft. In particular, I thank my interviewees who shared with me their perspectives, lives and experiences open heartedly. This work was supported by Zeit Foundation and German Research Foundation.

Notes

1. The data used in this article were collected for my doctoral project, which I concluded in 2012 and which was funded by the Settling Into Motion programme of the Ebelin and Gerd Bucerius *ZEIT* Foundation.
2. The nationality distribution was as follows: Belarus (1), Benin (1), Bulgaria (1), China (4), India (2), Israel (1), Jamaica (1), Japan (1), Kazakhstan (1), Kyrgyzstan (2), Macedonia (2), Malawi (1), Mexico (4), Netherlands (2), Nigeria (1), Philippines (1), Russia (3), Taiwan (2), Turkey (3) and Ukraine (1).
3. The main aim of this programme is to promote outstanding research, to transform graduate schools into internationally competitive centres of science and to advance the German academic and scientific environment (for more information see the website http://www.excellence-initiative.com of the German Research Council; on attracting international postgraduate students see the website http://www.research-in-germany.de of the Federal Ministry of Education).
4. All names used in this article are fictitious.
5. The numbers after the names correspond to the age of the interviewee.
6. This was particularly important to those Russian- and Spanish-speaking interviewees.

References

Basch, L., N. Glick-Schiller, and C. Szanton-Blanc. 1994. *Nations Unbound: Transnational Projects and Deterritorialized Nation-States*. Amsterdam: Overseas Publishers Association.

Bhabha, H. 1994a. "The Other Question: Stereotype, Discrimination and the Discourse of Colonialism." In *The Location of Culture*, edited by H. K. Bhabha, 94–120. London: Routledge.

Bhabha, H. 1994b. "Remembering Fanon: Self, Psyche and the Colonial Condition." In *Colonial Discourse and Post-Colonial Theory – a Reader*, edited by P. Williams and L. Chrisman, 112–123. New York: Columbia University Press.

Bilecen, B. 2009. "Lost in Status? Temporary, Permanent, Potential, Highly Skilled: The International Student Mobility." *COMCAD Working Papers* 63: 1–15.

Bilecen, B. 2012. "How Social Support Works among the Best and the Brightest: Evidence from International PhD Students in Germany." *Transnational Social Review – a Social Work Journal, Special Issue: Transnational Social Networks* 2 (2): 139–155.

Bochner, S., B. McLeod, and A. Lin. 1977. "Friendship Patterns of Overseas Students: A Functional Model." *International Journal of Psychology* 6 (3): 275–290.

Bolsmann, C., and H. Miller. 2008. "International Student Recruitment to Universities in England: Discourse, Rationales, and Globalisation." *Globalisation, Societies and Education* 6 (1): 75–88. doi:10.1080/14767720701855634.

Bourdieu, P. 1984. *Distinction: A Social Critique of the Judgement of Taste*. London: Routledge.

Bourdieu, P. 1985. "The Social Space and the Genesis of Groups." *Theory and Society* 14 (6): 723–744.

Bourdieu, P. 1989. "Social Space and Symbolic Power." *Sociological Theory* 7 (1): 14–25. doi:10.2307/202060.

Brooks, R., and J. Waters. 2011. *Student Mobilities, Migration and the Internationalization of Higher Education*. Basingstoke: Palgrave Macmillan. doi:10.1057/9780230305588.

Brown, L. 2009. "The Transformative Power of the International Sojourn: An Ethnographic Study of the International Student Experience." *Annals of Tourism Research* 36 (3): 502–521. doi:10.1016/j.annals.2009.03.002.

Brubaker, R., and F. Cooper. 2000. "Beyond Identity." *Theory and Society* 29 (1): 1–47. doi:10.1023/A:1007068714468.

Burr, V. 1995. *An Introduction to Social Constructionism*. London: Routledge. doi:10.4324/9780203299968.

Callero, P. L. 2003. "The Sociology of the Self." *Annual Review of Sociology* 29: 115–133. doi:10.1146/annurev.soc.29.010202.100057.

Clifford, J. 1997. *Routes: Travel and Translation in the Late Twentieth Century*. Cambridge, MA: Harvard University Press.

Faist, T. 2000. *The Volume and Dynamics of International Migration and Transnational Social Spaces*. Oxford: Oxford University Press. doi:10.1093/acprof:oso/9780198293910.001.0001.

Featherstone, M. 1995. *Undoing Culture: Globalization, Postmodernism and Identity*. London: Sage.

de Federico de la Rúa, A. 2007. "Networks and Identifications: A Relational Approach to Study Social Identities." *International Sociology* 22 (6): 683–699. doi:10.1177/0268580907082247.

Furnham, A., and N. Alibhai. 1985. "The Friendship Networks of Foreign Students: A Replication and Extension of the Functional Model." *International Journal of Psychology* 20 (3–4): 709–722. doi:10.1080/00207598508247565.

Furnham, A., and S. Bochner. 1986. *Culture Shock*. New York: Methuen.

Ghosh, S., and L. Wang. 2003. "Transnationalism and Identity: A Tale of Two Faces and Multiple Lives." *The Canadian Geographer* 47(3): 269–282. doi:10.1111/cag.2003.47.issue-3.

Gill, S. 2007. "Overseas Students' Intercultural Adaptation as Intercultural Learning: A Transformative Framework." *Compare: A Journal of Comparative and International Education* 37 (2): 167–183. doi:10.1080/03057920601165512.

Glick-Schiller, N., A. Caglar, and T. C. Guldbrandsen. 2006. "Beyond the Ethnic Lens: Locality, Globality and Born-Again Incorporation." *American Ethnologist* 33 (4): 612–633. doi:10.1525/ae.2006.33.issue-4.

Glick-Schiller, N., T. Darieva, and S. Gruner-Domic. 2011. "Defining Cosmopolitan Sociability in a Transnational Age. An Introduction." *Ethnic and Racial Studies* 34 (3): 399–418. doi:10.1080/01419870.2011.533781.

Gu, Q., M. Schweisfurth, and C. Day. 2010. "Learning and Growing in a 'Foreign' Context: Intercultural Experiences of International Students." *Compare: A Journal of Comparative and International Education* 40 (1): 7–23. doi:10.1080/03057920903115983.

Hall, S. 1990. "Cultural Identity and Diaspora." In *Identity: Community, Culture, Difference*, edited by J. Rutherford, 227–237. London: Lawrence & Wishart.

Hall, S. 1996. "Introduction: Who Needs 'Identity'?" In *Questions of Cultural Identity*, edited by S. Hall and P. Du Gay, 1–17. London: Sage.

Hannerz, U. 1990. "Cosmopolitans and Locals in World Culture." In *Global Culture: Nationalism, Globalization and Modernity*, edited by M. Featherstone, 237–252. London: Sage.

Hannerz, U. 1996. *Transnational Connections: Culture, People, Places*. London: Routledge.

Hayden, M. C., and J. J. Thompson. 1995. "Perceptions of International Education: A Preliminary Study." *International Review of Education* 41 (5): 389–404. doi:10.1007/BF01103036.

Hellstén, M., and A. Prescott. 2004. "Learning at University: The International Student Experience." *International Education Journal* 5 (3): 344–351.

Hsieh, H. F., and S. Shannon. 2005. "Three Approaches to Qualitative Content Analysis." *Qualitative Health Research* 15 (9): 1277–1288. doi:10.1177/1049732305276687.

Hsieh, M. 2006. "Identity Development of East Asian Female International Students with Implications for Second-Language Higher Education." *Education* 127 (1): 3–15.

Jenkins, R. 2008. *Social Identity*. 3rd ed. London and New York: Routledge.

King, R., and E. Ruiz-Gelices. 2003. "International Student Migration and the European 'Year Abroad': Effects on European Identity and Subsequent Migration Behaviour." *International Journal of Population Geography* 9 (3): 229–252. doi:10.1002/(ISSN)1099-1220.

Koehne, N. 2005. "(Re)Construction: Ways International Students Talk about Their Identity." *Australian Journal of Education* 49 (1): 104–119. doi:10.1177/000494410504900107.

Koehne, N. 2006. "(Be)Coming, (Be)Longing: Ways in Which International Students Talk about Themselves." *Discourse: Studies in Cultural Politics of Education* 27 (2): 241–257. doi:10.1080/01596300600676219.

Lalonde, R. N., D. M. Taylor, and F. M. Moghaddam. 1992. "The Process of Social Identification for Visible Immigrant Women in a Multicultural Setting." *Journal of Cross-Cultural Psychology* 23 (1): 25–39. doi:10.1177/002202219223 1002.

Lamont, M. 1992. *Money, Morals, & Manners. The Culture of the French and the American Upper-Middle Class*. Chicago, IL: The University of Chicago Press.

Lee, J., and C. Rice. 2007. "Welcome to America? International Student Perceptions of Discrimination." *Higher Education* 53 (3): 381–409. doi:10.1007/s10734-005-4508-3.

Liddicoat, A. J., C. Crozet, and J. Lo Bianco. 1999. "Striving for the Third Place: Consequences and Implications." In *Striving for the Third Place: Intercultural Competence through Language Education*, edited by J. Lo Bianco, A. J. Liddicoat, and C. Crozet, 1–20. Canberra: Language Australia.

Mau, S., J. Mewes, and A. Zimmermann. 2008. "Cosmopolitan Attitudes through Transnational Social Practices?" *Global Networks* 8 (1): 1–24.

Mayring, Ph. 2000. *Qualitative Inhaltsanalyse. Grundlagen Und Techniken* (7th ed., 1st ed. 1983). Weinheim: Deutscher Studien Verlag.

Merton, R. K. 1968. *Social Theory and Social Structure*. New York: Free Press.

Van Mol, C. 2011. "The Influence of European Student Mobility on European Identity and Subsequent Migration Behaviour." In *Analysing the Consequences of Academic Mobility and Migration*, edited by F. Dervin, 29–50. Newcastle: Cambridge Scholars Publishing.

Montgomery, C. 2010. *Understanding the International Student Experience*. Basingstoke: Palgrave Macmillan.

Murphy-Lejeune, E. 2002a. *Student Mobility and Narrative in Europe, The New Strangers*. London: Routledge.

Murphy-Lejeune, E. 2002b. "An Experience of Interculturality: Student Travellers." In *Intercultural Experience and Education*, edited by G. Alred, M. Byram, and M. Fleming, 101–113. Trowbridge, UK: Cromwell Press.

OECD (Organisation for Economic Co-operation and Development). 2012. "Education at a Glance 2012. OECD Indicators." OECD Publishing. http://dx.doi.org/10.1787/eag-2012-en

Rizvi, F. 2000. "International Education and the Production of a Global Imagination." In *Globalization and Education: Critical Perspectives*, edited by N. C. Burbules and C. A. Torres, 205–225. London: Routledge.

Rizvi, F. 2005. "International Education and the Production of Cosmopolitan Identities." A paper presented at the Transnational Seminar Series at the University of Illinois, Urbana-Champaign. https://www.ideals.illinois.edu/handle/2142/3516

Rizvi, F. 2010. "International Students and Doctoral Studies in Transnational Spaces." In *The Routledge Doctoral Supervisor's Companion: Supporting Effective Research in Education and the Social Sciences*, edited by M. Walker and P. Thompson, 158–170. London and New York: Routledge.

Robertson, S. 2011. "Cash Cows, Backdoor Migrants, or Activist Citizens? International Students, Citizenship, and Rights in Australia." *Ethnic and Racial Studies* 34 (12): 2192–2211. doi:10.1080/01419870.2011.558590.

Robinson-Pant, A. 2005. *Cross-Cultural Perspectives on Educational Research*. Buckingham: Open University Press.

Robinson-Pant, A. 2009. "Changing Academies: Exploring International PhD Students' Perspectives on 'Host' and 'Home' Universities." *Higher Education Research and Development* 28 (4): 417–429.

Samuelowicz, K. 1987. "Learning Problems of Overseas Students: Two Sides of a Story." *Higher Education Research and Development* 6 (2): 121–133.

Schmitt, M. T., R. Spears, and N. R. Branscombe. 2002. "Constructing a Minority Group Identity out of Shared Rejection: The Case of International Students." *European Journal of Social Psychology* 33 (1): 1–12.

Singh, M., F. Rizvi, and M. Shrestha. 2007. "Student Mobility and the Spacial Production of Cosmopolitan Identities." In *Spatial Theories of Education: Policy and Geography Matters*, edited by K. N. Gulson and C. Symes, 195–214. New York: Routledge.

Stromquist, N. P., and K. Monkman. 2000. "Defining Globalization and Assessing Its Implications on Knowlege and Education." In *Globalization and Education: Integration and Contestation across Cultures*, edited by N. P. Stromquist and K. Monkman, 3–26. Lanham, MD: Rowman & Littlefield.

Tajfel, H., and J. C. Turner. 1979. "An Integrative Theory of Social Conflict." In *The Social Psychology of Intergroup Relations*, edited by S. Worchel and W. Austin, 33–47. Monterey, CA: Brooks-Cole Publishers.

Thorsby, C. D. 1991. "The Financial Impact of Foreign Student Enrollments." *Higher Education* 21 (3): 351–358. doi:10.1007/BF00132725.

Tian, M., and J. Lowe. 2009. "Existentialist Internationalization and the Chinese Student Experience in English Universities." *Compare: A Journal of Comparative and International Education* 39 (5): 659–676. doi:10.1080/03057920903125693.

Tomlinson, M. 2003. "Lifestyle and Social Class." *European Sociological Review* 19 (1): 97–111. doi:10.1093/esr/19.1.97.

Torres, V., S. R. Jones, and K. A. Renn. 2009. "Identity Development Theories in Student Affairs: Origins, Current Status, and New Approaches." *Journal of College Student Development* 50 (6): 577–596. doi:10.1353/csd.0.0102.

Trotter, E., and C. A. Roberts. 2006. "Enhancing the Early Student Experience." *Higher Education Research & Development* 25 (4): 371–386.

Valenta, M. 2009. "Immigrants' Identity Negotiations and Coping with Stigma in Different Relational Frames." *Symbolic Interaction* 32 (4): 351–371. doi:10. 1525/si.2009.32.4.351.

Vertovec, S., and R. Cohen, eds. 2002. *Conceiving Cosmopolitanism. Theory, Context and Practice*. Oxford: Oxford University Press.

Werbner, P. 1997. "Essentialising Essentialism, Essentialising Silence: Ambivalence and Multiplicity in the Constructions of Racism and Ethnicity." In *Debating Cultural Hybridity: Multi-Cultural Identities and the Politics of Anti-Racism*, edited by P. Werbner and T. Modood, 226–254. London: Zed Books.

'Selective cosmopolitans': tutors' and students' experience of offshore higher education in Dubai

Laila Kadiwal[a] and Irfan A. Rind[b]

[a]School of Law, Politics and Sociology, University of Sussex, Brighton, UK; [b]Department of Education Management, Sukkur Institute of Business Administration, Sukkur, Pakistan

As the offshore mobility of higher education has increased in recent times, the question of how it interacts with the recipient cultures has become ever more significant. Using ethnographic methods, this empirical study examined the adaptation of the UK teacher education model – the Postgraduate Certificate in Education – to the context of Dubai. The study asks 'how do students and tutors experience the adaptation of British education in the context of Dubai?' This paper will argue that tutors and students in offshore Dubai teacher education are 'selective cosmopolitans' who negotiate cross-cultural influences pragmatically and ambivalently. The study addresses a significant gap in the literature, as there is little written on the internationalisation of higher education in the context of Gulf Cooperation Council countries. There is also an inadequate appreciation of the role of local culture and religion in offshore education and tutors and students' role as active agents in negotiating cross-cultural dynamics in the offshore educational setting.

Introduction

The paper explores the experiences of tutors and students engaged in an offshore educational programme in Dubai. Within the context of higher education internationalisation, 'offshore education' describes the situation where an educational provider moves across borders to offer programmes in a host country (Davis, Olsen, and Böhm 2000). Thus, offshore education provides students with the opportunity to earn foreign qualifications without having to leave their home countries (McBurnie and Pollock 2000). It is delivered in various formats, from twinning arrangements through to franchising, moderated programs and online education to branch campuses (Hayes and Wynyard 2002). Offshore education has been growing at

123

between 3% and 5% per year since the year 2000 and its importance is likely to increase in the coming years (Centre for International Economics 2008).

Mary Louise Pratt's (1991) concept of the 'contact zone' provides this study with a key theoretical underpinning. In her influential paper 'Arts of the Contact Zone' Pratt speaks of contact zones as, 'social spaces where cultures meet, clash and grapple with each other, often in contexts of highly asymmetrical relations of power …' (1) This concept is further developed by Singh and Doherty (2004) who expand it to 'global contact zones', to include sites of international higher education where individuals come with diverse worldviews, histories and educational experiences and contest cross-cultural dilemmas. Developing this concept still further, this paper contributes to our understanding of international tutors and students as 'selective cosmopolitans' who negotiate the central tensions around language and culture pragmatically and ambivalently in the contact zone that is offshore education in Dubai. In our usage of the term 'selective cosmopolitans', we refer to individuals who, in order to advantageously position themselves in the contemporary globalised world, negotiate between different cultural influences pragmatically, while simultaneously experiencing ambivalence and tensions in terms of their sense of identity. These individuals are inherently reflexive regarding the unavoidable complexity of their situation.

Crucially, this research will focus on the perceptions of participants in offshore education – teachers and students. Teachers are at the forefront of confronting ethical and cultural dilemmas on behalf of their institutions as they navigate between upholding the ethics of cultural respect on the one hand, and providing a linguistic and cultural acculturation towards Western education on the other. Nor should students be regarded as passive recipients of a service, as is often the case in the didactic, tutor-centred model of 'traditional' education in the Gulf Cooperation Council (GCC) region – rather they should be seen as, 'active agents purposefully and advantageously imagining and positioning themselves in global flows … to their advantage' (Singh and Doherty 2004, 36).

This research was conducted at an institution we will refer to as UK University (UKU) in Dubai. The UKU adapted the UK Postgraduate Certificate in Education (PGCE) in collaboration with a Russell Group British university to train teachers in teaching English-medium mathematics and science in Dubai state schools. Data were generated through in-depth semi-structured interviews and focus groups with students and teachers.

The paper makes an important contribution to the field of knowledge by adding information on the impact of internationalisation of higher education in the United Arab Emirates (UAE) and cultural negotiations involved in offshore education. Miller-Idriss and Hanauer (2011), who have traced the reasons for the rapid growth of transnational higher education in the Arab states, observe that virtually nothing has been written on the effects that offshore campuses are having on local cultures and identities in the GCC region. Moreover, the current literature on offshore education sheds little light on the agency of tutors and students.

The following section discusses the key literature and debates in offshore education. This will be followed by an overview of the relationship between the UK and Dubai as the provider and receiver of offshore education, situating the research question in this context. The article will then describe theories of cosmopolitanism relevant to understanding tutors' and students' engagement in offshore education. After outlining the research design, the article will illustrate the pragmatic and ambivalent way in which the participants negotiate their cosmopolitan identities. The article concludes with broader reflections and the limitations of the study.

Globalisation, internationalisation and offshore higher education

Internationalisation has become a widespread phenomenon in higher education since the 1990s. According to Teichler (2004), 'internationalisation [of education is] a trend or policy direction away from a more or less closed national system of higher education' (6). Altbach and Knight (2007) provide a useful distinction between globalisation and internationalisation: 'Globalization is the context of economic and academic trends that are part of the reality of the twenty-first century', while 'internationalisation includes the policies and practices undertaken by academic systems and institutions – and even individuals – to cope with the global academic environment' (290). Thus, within higher education, globalisation is the context and internationalisation is the policy and practice-based outcome.

Within this context, offshore education can be seen as one area of activity within a wider internationalisation agenda. The following section examines the status of current scholarship on offshore education.

Offshore education: an under-researched area of international education

The crucial issue with the current literature on international education is that offshore education has been treated as a peripheral subject. The existing literature on international education can be divided into four categories. The first type focuses on its economic dimension (e.g. Massey et al. 1994; Marginson and Rhoades 2002; Sajitha 2007; Kauppinen 2012). Such studies examine how transnational academic mobility is shaped by neo-liberal policies. The second type of study investigates students' experiences in international education. Many of these discuss the experiences of students from around the world coming to English-speaking countries for study (e.g. Ballard and Clanchy 1997; Andrade 2006; Brown 2009; Schweisfurth and Gu 2009; Briguglio and Smith 2012; Oikonomidoy and Williams 2013). A few of these studies focus on the experiences of students travelling from English-speaking countries for the purpose of education (e.g. Jones 2010;

Waters, Brooks, and Pimlott-Wilson 2011). The third type of study focuses on the experiences of academics in international education. Some examine the difficulties that academics from non-English-speaking backgrounds encounter in English-speaking universities (e.g. Debowski 2003; Leask et al. 2005). Other studies focus on the challenges encountered by academics from English-speaking countries in offshore teaching (e.g. Gribble and Ziguras 2003; Dunn and Wallace 2006; Poole and Ewan 2010). The fourth type of study evaluates the organisational dimensions of internationalisation, such as the nature of partnerships and policies (e.g. Gainey and Andressen 2002; Heffernan and Poole 2005; McBurnie and Ziguras 2007; Ryan 2011).

Most of the studies mentioned above are primarily grounded in the contexts and experiences of the West. As a result, knowledge of offshore education is limited in terms of issues and settings explored. The small body of existing literature on offshore education primarily revolves around Hong Kong, Indonesia, South Korea and Singapore (Burden-Leahy 2009). These studies mainly explore students' satisfaction and challenges that academics and students face. For instance, Chapman and Pyvis (2006a, 2006b), and Pyvis and Chapman (2007) examine students' experiences in Australian offshore education in Malaysia, Singapore and Hong Kong. They highlight students' dilemmas in developing a sense of belonging to the academic community, meeting educational goals and adjusting to differences in teaching styles. Dobos (2011) investigates the challenges faced by academic staff based in an offshore Australian university in Malaysia in terms of workload issues and lack of equivalent recognition to their Australian counterparts. However, there is little literature focusing on the relationship between students' cultural or religious identities and their learning experiences in offshore education. Having explored the general literature on offshore education, this paper will now focus on the limitations of existing scholarship on international education in the UAE.

Offshore education research in the context of the UAE

There is a small body of literature on the internationalisation of higher education in the context of the UAE. For example, Burden-Leahy (2009) has assessed the economic, social and political impact of globalisation on the UAE's higher education. Smith (2009) examined the experience of academics based in an offshore campus in Dubai in terms of quality assurance. Wilkins, Balakrishnan, and Huisman (2012) have investigated students' perceptions of studying at international branch campuses in the UAE. However, none of these studies analyse the cultural tensions faced by academics and students in offshore education.

Lane (2011) has discussed International Branch Campuses (IBC) in Dubai from a policy perspective. He argues that Dubai is purposefully recruiting IBCs from different countries as a way of providing expatriates and their children with an education familiar to them and to respond to the demand for an overseas education. Another study, by Miller-Idriss and Hanauer (2011), mapped the reasons for the rapid growth of transnational higher education in the Arab states. Wilkins (2001b) has argued that Western education is highly valued in the UAE. In his survey, 62% of respondents believed that the UK offers the best higher education worldwide. These studies explain the contemporary demand of offshore educational models in the context of the UAE. However, they ignore the cultural impact of the adaptation of offshore models.

Findlow (2008) has explored the ways in which the Middle East has long engaged with secular models of education, thereby challenging the essentialist distinction between Islamic states as 'fundamentalist' and the rest of the world as largely 'secular'. Crabtree's (2010) study on how she adapted an American liberal arts course at a public university in the UAE is relevant to this paper. Her focus is on describing the innovative pedagogy that she used as she asked students to investigate their own setting. However, she does not reflect on the challenges or dilemmas that she or her students encountered in adapting the foreign curriculum in the local scenario. None of these studies recognise that there is a dialectical relationship between religious and cultural norms and offshore education. This very important issue of cross-cultural dynamics, which is mostly ignored in the UAE, has been raised in other settings. For instance, while Wang (2007) investigates differences in perceptions of leadership in the USA and China in an offshore MBA programme, Ng (2012) makes a theoretical claim for the respect for local cultures in offshore education in the South Pacific.

The idea of the adaptation of offshore education to the local context has been problematised by scholars such as Pyvis and Chapman (2007) and Ziguras (1999). On one hand, there are arguments against indiscriminate use of Western ideas in non-Western settings (Wang 2007); on the other hand, Pyvis and Chapman (2007) have argued that it denies students the opportunity to discover Western concepts and ways of thinking, which is one of the reasons why they enrol at offshore campuses. Ziguras (1999) has remarked that offshore courses are increasingly offered to students from many nations, making responsiveness to local cultures difficult.

Having reviewed current issues and trends in offshore education and focused discussion on the UAE, the next section of this paper will elaborate on the global role of the UK and Dubai in offshore education.

The asymmetrical positions of the UK and Dubai in offshore education

The UK and Dubai stand on two different extremes of a continuum as an exporter and an importer of international education.

The UK as an exporter of international higher education

Higher education institutes (HEIs) are one of the UK's fastest growing sources of export earnings. The overall value of their international activities is expected to rise from £14.1 billion in 2008–2009 to £26.6 billion by 2025 (Conlon, Litchfield, and Sadlier 2011, 9). In 2007, the UK was the second top destination for international students after the USA (Straw 2011). The UK is home to three of the world's most prestigious higher education institutions. According to the Higher Education Statistics Agency (2009), 196,640 offshore students were studying in 112 of the UK's HEIs during the 2007–2008 academic year, earning the sector over £268 million. More than half of these offshore students were on distance learning courses, while others were at overseas campuses run by either British universities or foreign partners. Nearly 23% of students were in the European Union and 45% studied in Asia. Hong Kong, Singapore, Malaysia and China accounted for 37% of total offshore provision between them.

There are several providers of British education in Dubai, such as the University of Birmingham, Bradford University, City University, the University of Edinburgh, the University of Exeter, Middlesex University and the University of Sunderland. Their programmes range from one to four years and include courses such as engineering, computer science, fashion, media studies, environmental studies, child development and business management.

Dubai as an importer of international higher education

Dubai has attempted to position itself as the regional hub of international higher education in the Middle East. Of the estimated 100 offshore campuses and programmes currently operating worldwide, over one-third are in the Middle East. The UAE alone houses 61% of the region's transnational educational arrangements (Miller-Idriss and Hanauer 2011). As of the data available from 2010, Dubai had 27 regional and international universities from 11 different countries, which was the largest number in any one location in the world. Together they catered to over 20,000 students from 137 nationalities through over 400 higher education programmes (Dubai International Academic City 2013). Dubai has established the world's first and only free zone area for higher education, allowing overseas institutions 100% ownership, 100% freedom from taxes and 100% repatriation of profits.

Dubai's international education is shaped by three crucial factors (Dubai Strategic Plan 2015). Firstly, there is a recognition that Dubai needs to develop its capacity to compete in the global economy. This is considered extremely important as Dubai's oil resources are rapidly depleting. Secondly, there is a federal government strategy to equip UAE nationals with employable skills. Large numbers of nationals are unemployed due to a lack of these skills (Wilkins 2001a). Thirdly, there is a large market of expatriate students seeking higher education as Dubai's population consists of roughly 87% expatriates (Dubai Statistics Centre 2009).

Internationalisation: on whose terms?

Since the UK and Dubai stand on opposite sides of a continuum as exporter and importer of offshore education, the question is who is leading the internationalisation?

Connell (2007) contends that Eurocentric assumptions and their assumed superiority drive the internationalisation processes in the world. Phillipson (1992) calls this a form of cultural and linguistic imperialism. The English language is seen as a language of elitism, power and prosperity. The significance of English is increasingly established in the academic, scientific and technological sectors globally (Böhm et al. 2004). MacKinnon and Manathunga (2003) argue that Western universities tend to assume that it is the non-Western populations that need to learn from the West.

Dubai has increasingly looked to the West for transforming its higher education system in the last two decades. When the first university was founded in 1977, Dubai drew upon expertise from Egypt and other Arab states. The medium of instruction and scholarship was Arabic. Now it is the Western experts, Western education and English language that pervade Dubai's educational landscape.

This raises another question: what does internationalisation mean for Arabic language, culture and society? The business of exporting or importing higher education is not only an act of exchanging educational products, but also of ensuring the flow of ideologies, social values and cultural symbols (Rizvi 2010). Miller-Idriss and Hanauer (2011) raise the issue of Westernisation in the context of the Middle East. They argue that there is a need to research and share ordinary people's voices and demonstrate the impact that such campuses are having on local culture.

In the light of this need, this paper will attempt to make sense of the impact that offshore education has had on the local culture and identity through the perspective of academics and students involved in offshore education. The following section explains the theoretical framework used to interpret their voices.

Theoretical framework: cosmopolitan engagement

This study draws upon cosmopolitan theory to understand students' and tutors' experiences of engaging with offshore education in the context of Dubai. There is little consensus on exactly what cosmopolitanism is. Most authors, however, agree that 'cosmopolitans espouse a broadly defined disposition of openness toward others, people, things and experiences whose origin is non-local' (Skrbis and Woodward 2007, 730). Based on a comprehensive literature review by Beck and Sznaider (2006) and Fine (2006), there appear two prominent trends in the discourse of cosmopolitanism. The first trend is rooted in ancient Greek philosophy, which considers our collective humanity as more important than any other collective identity. The term cosmopolitan itself derives from the Greek *kosmopolites* meaning 'citizen of the world' (Hansen 2008, 290). It is a moral and political ideal. The second trend refers to a cultural process of 'cosmopolitanisation' of society, and has been developed through the works of Giddens (1999), Beck (2002), Held (2002), Urry (2003) and Calhoun (2006). There are several ways to describe how people negotiate the global-local dichotomy. Empirical studies have generated numerous concepts such as 'mundane cosmopolitanism' (Urry 2000), 'working class cosmopolitans' (Werbner 1999) and 'global looking localists' (Philips 2002). Delanty (2006) calls this diversity of conceptions a 'plurality of cosmopolitan projects' (35).

International higher education as a space of cosmopolitan engagement

Mobility is central to making international education a space of cosmopolitan experiences. Individuals accumulate cosmopolitan dispositions through study abroad, international work, transnational networks of friends and the mastery of English and other foreign languages (Weenink 2008). Many theorists propose that contemporary education should cultivate a cosmopolitan sensibility. Nussbaum (1997) argues that education should instil a philosophical outlook that each of us is part of a common humanity. Noddings (2005) recommends that it should cultivate values such as mutual respect, appreciation for diversity and social justice. Gardiner (2006) proposes that education should provide skills to work collaboratively with people from diverse backgrounds and of diverse intelligence. These approaches mainly offer generalised and highly abstract conceptions. We need paradigms and vocabulary to make sense of everyday cosmopolitan experiences of academic community in international higher education (Rizvi 2005).

Selective cosmopolitans: the theoretical concept explained

The concept 'selective cosmopolitans' draws its inspiration from Skrbis and Woodward's (2007) 'strategic' and 'ambivalent' cosmopolitans to understand how students and tutors engage with offshore education in Dubai. According to Skrbis and Woodward, people are 'strategic' cosmopolitans because they discursively participate in being cosmopolitan. Cosmopolitanism is 'not an ideal type but a negotiated frame of reference for dealing with cultural differences' (730). Cosmopolitan values are not seen as expressed fully at all times and on all issues. Weenink (2008) identifies two types of cosmopolitans: 'dedicated' and 'pragmatic' cosmopolitans. Dedicated cosmopolitans demonstrate a commitment to being world citizens.

They are willing to look beyond borders out of their genuine interest in others. Contrarily, pragmatic cosmopolitans would consider looking beyond borders if there were opportunities for their own progress. Skrbis and Woodward (2007) define 'ambivalence' as 'tensions which are tolerated' and they 'constitute background awareness of inevitable complexities of a situation' (746). The above concepts have contributed to the theoretical framework developed to interpret students' and teachers' experiences in the offshore education setting of Dubai. The term selective cosmopolitans describes individuals who are keen to advantageously position themselves in the contemporary globalised world. While doing so they negotiate between different cultural influences pragmatically, simultaneously experiencing ambivalence and tensions in terms of their sense of identity. These individuals are, 'not the dupes of overpowering social structures and events but active reflective agents in the ongoing construction of social reality' (Cameron and Block 2002, 4). In the following section, we will discuss the way we collected data for this study.

Methodology

This ethnographic research was conducted at the Dubai campus of a university we shall call 'UKU', one of several providers of British education in Dubai. The UKU launched the British teacher education model of the PGCE in Dubai. In this context, the following research questions were asked:

- How do students and tutors experience the adaptation of the UK's teacher education model in the context of Dubai?
- What do they view as the challenges and benefits of the adaptation of the UK model?

The research participants for the study were sampled from the second cohort of PGCE students who were in progress at the time of the study. The programme was taught by four tutors, all of whom are referred to below by pseudonyms:

- Radha, from the Far East, and Nicola, from Europe, were training students in teaching English language.
- Bilal, from the Middle East, was involved training students to teach science.
- Peter, from Europe, was teaching students how to teach mathematics in state schools.

These tutors came from diverse faiths, national and cultural backgrounds. They had previously worked in countries such as the USA, the UK, Singapore and Yemen.

The cohort had 11 students (also referred to as trainee-teachers to distinguish them from state school pupils). Out of six females and five males, five female and three male students participated in the study. All of them identified themselves as Muslims, 10 of them were Arab and they hailed from countries such as Egypt, Syria, Jordan, Palestine, Tunisia, Iraq and Lebanon. The only Hispanic trainee-teacher, Maryam, a fluent Arabic and English speaker, was from North America.

Since the study primarily focused on the experiences of the tutors and trainee-teachers, it inevitably necessitated a qualitative and interpretive research design. It was concerned 'with understanding what other human beings are doing or saying' (Schwandt 2000, 200). Consequently, the main method of collecting data from tutors was in-depth and semi-structured interviews. The interviews focused on the way they appropriated material from the British context to serve the needs of Dubai and the tensions and challenges that they faced in the process.

Focus groups were used as the main method of data collection from trainee-teachers. Two focus groups were conducted for male and female trainee-teachers separately as they preferred to dialogue in same-gender groups. These focus groups generated rich and lively data through participants exchanging experiences and anecdotes and commenting on each other's views (Kitzinger 1995, 299). Since English was their second language for a majority of them, they also helped each other to express themselves.

In addition, documents were reviewed to obtain factual understanding and background to the programme. Data were also collected through participation in three departmental meetings, observation of four teaching-learning activities and several informal interactions with students and tutors over a period of four weeks. These strategies helped in making better sense of what the participants had said in their interviews and focus groups. Together these methods – interviews, focus groups, documents and observation – not only helped to triangulate the information to ensure validity, but also contributed to a deeper understanding of the participants' experiences.

Since the epistemological paradigm of the study suggests a possibility of multiple truths, validity depends on reliable interpretation of data. In a qualitative study, 'one validates not a test but an interpretation of data arising from a specified procedure' (Cronbach 1971, 447). Therefore, Miles and Huberman's (2002) 'fairly classic set' of procedures, as described by Punch (2005, 194), were followed. We used the 'data reduction', 'data display' and 'drawing and verifying conclusions' techniques. We reduced data through editing and summarising, labelled pieces of data and identified patterns and relationships between them. We also reflected on the deeper concepts that possibly underpinned the codes. During this process, a major challenge was ensuring that there was no significant loss of information and data was not deprived of its context. Using the techniques of data display, we ordered pieces of the data in a logical flow and kept changing their places as the data analysis progressed. This was not a linear process. We kept drawing conclusions and verifying them. As recurring themes emerged, the key issues experienced by tutors and students in the adaptation of offshore education came to the fore.

Findings: selective and ambivalent cosmopolitans

The study investigated how international tutors and Arab students engaged with the adaptation of the offshore education in the context of Dubai. Findings suggest that tutors and students, as selective cosmopolitans, negotiated the central tensions around language and culture pragmatically and ambivalently in their offshore education experience.

Linguistic negotiations: a space for both – English and Arabic

The issue of language is not separate from that of culture, but it has been discussed here separately because the Arabic-English debate emerged as critical in the process of the adaptation of the UK model. The UKU's initial aim of adapting the UK's teacher education programme for Dubai was to train teachers in teaching mathematics and science through the medium of the English language. This was based on the UAE federal government's decision to replace Arabic with English language as a medium of instructions for mathematics and science in state schools. When the first two cohorts of PGCE graduates went into UAE state schools to practice teaching mathematics through the medium of English, they faced resistance from pupils, their parents and the school administration. Questions about the status of Arabic as a serious language of scholarship and Arab identity were raised. The matter escalated and the government rescinded the decision.

Against this backdrop, the tutors and trainee-teachers clearly experienced tensions around the issue of language. On one hand, they valued the English language as a passport to global mobility and economic development, and a practical necessity; on the other hand, they saw it as a threat to Arabic and, by extension, a threat to their religious and cultural identity. Maha, a trainee-teacher from Lebanon, confided[1]:

> We need to be realistic that the world around us is using English everywhere and we need to make students and schools as I told you understand [this]. Knowledge has to be applicable so we have to use English.

Karim, a Jordanian trainee-teacher, stressed that it was important to 'help them [state school pupils] to improve English language so that they could face life'. Mitsikopoulou (2007, 232) analyses two main discourses concerning English language: the first is 'progress and development' discourse and the second is 'cosmopolitan discourse' with an international, outward-looking orientation. If this framework is used, the tutors and students clearly partici-

133

pated in 'progress and development' discourse. Reema, from Palestine, argued:

> If we are not going to use English in all subjects they [students] will stay low. If you are going to use Arabic all the time they will not develop. We need to use English. They will develop little by little their level of English.

While they valued English language as a necessity they also saw it as a threat to their religious and cultural identity. The following is an excerpt from the focus group:

> Karim: So we have to teach in English. Yes, they have strong point of view but I think that point of view will destroy the main point of view, which is Arabic.

> Ehsan: They want to make Dubai an emerging or an English-medium place. But that will destroy; will hide another main thing in our lives, which is Arabic language. We use it when we socialise, when we pray for example Quran.

They deeply valued Arabic as integral to their religious and cultural identity. It was seen as holding the symbolic capital of the Quran (Vaish 2008, 463). Trainee-teachers explained:

> Ehsan: I mean you know our language is very important part of our lives. If you don't speak Arabic or read Arabic that means you … lost half of the things. You don't understand your identity.

> Adnan: Then, we are not Arabs any more, *khalas* [finished]!

Their ambivalence was about how to establish the roles of both languages in an educational setting, without the one compromising the other. There was no either/or. As 'selective cosmopolitans', the Arab students, and also their Arab tutor, sought to address this dilemma by recommending the use of bilingual teaching in public schools. Some trainee-teachers suggested that English should be the primary medium of instruction and only when children did not understand in English should the teacher resort to Arabic. Others recommended subject-wise division of English and Arabic. They suggested that mathematics and science could be taught in English and the subjects connected with identity and culture such as history and geography should be taught in Arabic. Some of them suggested mixed-language use. They believed that terminologies should stay in English and their explanation should be offered in Arabic. They considered that certain terminologies were difficult to translate in Arabic and some concepts were difficult to explain in English. Ehsan, a trainee-teacher, justified this with his experience:

I remember in college, one of the doctors was Arabic. She wanted to teach us a concept. She was speaking in English and repeating and repeating for one hour, come from here and there and we were not able to understand what she was talking about and then suddenly she decided to say it in Arabic. And when she said that, all of us 'Yeah, ahhh, OK.' ...Mix Arabic and English, so it will be the best, we can get the idea 100%.

Bilal, the Arab tutor, considered bilingualism as necessary to teach science:

Language is the major thing. Public schools really do not emphasise the English language that much, so teaching of sciences in those schools is really problematic.... You really have to understand both languages.

The three non-Arab tutors and Maryam, the only non-Arab trainee-teacher, supported the use of Arabic as the primary medium of instruction in schools. Maryam argued against bilingual teaching because it affected not only students' learning but also their native culture:

First of all you have to consider the students. They are underachievers in their own language. If you teach them in English, they, I don't feel, will learn too much. I feel that English will replace their native language. They are going to lose their native language and culture.

Some of the students and tutors also argued that the implicit idea behind replacing Arabic with English is that somehow Arabic is not a suitable vehicle for the expression of basic mathematics. Not only is this false, but it cripples students' ability to use Arabic creatively, thereby establishing a dependency relationship. They proposed alternative ways of teaching English. Radha, the English tutor, recommended:

To bring up the importance of English they don't have to switch the curriculum, all they need to do is to focus on the syllabus of English and I don't think they should start imposing English on other subjects. ... I think the perception of English as the main language here has to change.

While the tutors and trainee-teachers seemed to respond pragmatically to the issue of language as discussed above, their stance appeared to be marked by ambivalence and contradictions. As defined above, 'ambivalence' refers to tensions that are tolerated and they constitute background awareness of inevitable complexities of a situation (Skrbis and Woodward 2007, 746). The non-Arabic tutors strongly supported the use of Arabic, but did not make an effort to learn it themselves and continued to prepare students to teach these subjects in English. Though the Arab trainee-teachers feared the impact of English on their identity and culture, they had enrolled into the programme that aimed to replace Arabic as a medium of instruction with English. When asked which language the trainee teachers preferred to teach mathematics and science in school, even those who had supported

Arabic as the central medium of instruction acknowledged that they had found it easier to teach in English than in Arabic. Some of the trainee teachers, however, were willing to teach in Arabic for mainly identity reasons. Saif, a mathematics trainee, said:

> I wouldn't mind at all because my mother tongue is Arabic. Some pupils will come and embarrass us. 'Where do you come from? Oh, you are an Arabi! Then why don't you speak in Arabic? Why are you teaching in English, you are an Arabi.'

Overall, the tutors and trainee-teachers can be seen as selective cosmopolitans, who valued English as the language for academic, economic and global mobility, while situating Arabic primarily as the marker of Arab identity and religion. Eventually, the programme adapted to bilingual teaching in state schools as a result of resistance from parents and schools to English-medium teaching of Mathematics and Science subjects. The original imperative of the offshore education to replace Arabic with English in the teaching of mathematics and science could be seen as un-cosmopolitan. However, the very idea of adaptation meant cosmopolitan openness to negotiate with the local context.

Having discussed the issue of language, we will now turn to the related field of culture.

The cultural politics of cosmopolitan negotiations

The findings show that the local cultural norms and religion played a significant role in the adaptation of the offshore model in the context of Dubai and had an impact on students' learning. It involved cultural negotiations in the delivery of the curriculum. Skrbis and Woodward (2007) suggest that the availability of a vast supermarket of goods, images and services that can be accessed locally, inevitably involves cultural politics of selection and rejection of products.

The tutors and trainee-teachers saw overseas education as an opportunity to participate in globalisation. They considered it as qualitatively better than the local education and appreciated its 'student-centred teaching-learning methods'. They labelled it as 'modern', 'effective', 'new' and 'relevant'. Trainee-teachers also saw it as an opportunity to learn from others. The following is an excerpt from the trainee-teachers' focus group on what they perceived to be the usefulness of offshore education:

> Maha: If UAE wants more learner-centred classroom then they have solved this problem through offering offshore education.

> Leena: Yeah, offshore education offers modern classrooms.

Fiza: In fact, [it is] something that should have come years ago. It is useful because we need to interact with each other.

Leena: Yeah, it is an opportunity. We need to be open. We need to learn from other countries.

According to Parry (2007), openness is partly a product of an ideology of progress. As with Chapman and Pyvis's (2007) findings in Hong Kong, Malaysia and Singapore, enrolling into international education was a deliberate and informed strategy of the students. It signified quality and status and contributing to international exposure and outlook. It was also considered an investment in career advancement.

Thus, while trainee-teachers had positive views about English-language-based 'offshore' education, they had selectively negotiated certain of its cultural implications. For instance, trainee-teachers saw the gender policies of the programme as different from their traditional cultural values. Most trainee-teachers had previously studied in gender-segregated classes and had grown up in an environment where equality between men and women was conceived differently from the way it was implicit in the programme, which had provided them with a mixed-gender learning environment. They appreciated this sense of equality, but adapted it within their cultural sensibilities. They participated in collaborative or peer learning activities within same-sex groups and socialised within same-sex groups. The tutors adapted to this in their teaching practice. Even the research method for this research needed to be changed: instead of conducting one mixed-gender focus group as originally planned, two separate focus groups for male and female trainee-teachers were administered.

While cultural differences around gender-relations were negotiated relatively easily, trainee-teachers found certain theoretical constructs more difficult to negotiate, such as the concept of probability in mathematics:

Saif: One of the terms we have to teach is probability and we have to throw that dice. I think those are not accepted in Islam because it's like *bidun* [forbidden]. There is no luck. There is nothing like luck in Islam, we call it fate.

Ehsan: There are semi-sensitive topics and we don't like to talk about it. If teacher discusses this issue, this will affect our religious identity.

Adnan: So we cannot give them those opinions in schools. But we can take. Of course they have other good opinions for example Piaget or Marx. Anyone who has good opinions we can take the good things and teach the students … for us we have to learn both opinions.

Ehsan: I think even we don't need to learn these opinions. Why should I know something against my belief?

This shows that students were open to learning new perspectives, but resisted those that challenged their deeply-held religious or cultural beliefs.

The tutors modified the UK-derived curriculum to make it more culturally sensitive. Nicola remarked, 'What students cannot relate to, doesn't work'. Radha described:

> I wouldn't introduce anything that involves going to the pubs or alcohol, anything like that at all, or say, a scenario in which a boy meets the girl. Because there is no point, they can't relate to it. This is why some of the published materials are completely inappropriate ... I am not looking to get anti-response from them. Just something more realistic, something they are happy to deal with.

Bilal, the Science tutor, spoke about how he strategically created culturally appropriate experiences to enhance trainee-teachers' learning:

> Environmental issues are culturally connected, you can't bring in examples of the USA; you need to bring in desert culture here in environmental issues, for example, water quality testing. I capitalize on salt water, mineral water, some students have been to Mecca, Zamzam water. ... So you really need to connect the students to that [their culture] and then add another layer to it, of science.

Bilal carefully taught the course as he felt that certain aspects of the curriculum were sensitive to the beliefs of the participants:

> Science itself is really very critical area ... you need to be really very objective in science that you don't need to rely on some superior authority, and so that thing [religion] itself needs to be like brought in very, very carefully.

The cultural adaptation of the offshore model inevitably gave rise to debates and ambiguity on what culturally appropriate was and the place of religion in the programme. To illustrate these points, we draw upon the policy of wearing the *abaya* [full-length gown], which had become a source of contention. Public schools required female teachers to cover their heads with a scarf and wear the *abaya*. The female trainee-teachers' views differed on the style of *abaya*. When a non-Arab tutor commented on an Arab female trainee-teacher Lena's *abaya* as tight and thus culturally inappropriate for public school, she resisted. In Lebanon, she was used to a different interpretation of modesty than the one she encountered on the programme. Lena protested, 'I don't wear *abaya*. It is not religion, it's tradition, local culture. It's not my culture.' Instances like these challenged a homogenous picture of Islam and Arab culture. In another major instance, in the first cohort, one of the two Arab-Christian students refused to wear the *abaya*, stating that she had not enrolled into the programme as Muslim so she would not abide by the rule. Consequently, there were no Christian trainee-teachers in the next cohort. Nicola shared her observation:

Actually in the first cohort there were two Christian students in the course. One of the students objected strongly to being asked to wear *abaya* and scarf on the grounds that she enrolled into the programme as a Christian. In this particular cohort everybody is covered so there isn't problem. There is one student whose dress is rather inappropriate … even though she is veiled her dress is quite tight.

These examples demonstrate that the local culture and religion played a role in the adaptation of the offshore model in the context of Dubai.

Trainee-teachers were open to learning from international tutors irrespective of their backgrounds, as long as they were sensitive to the students' cultural and religious perspectives. One of the conversations with the students occurred as follows:

Adnan: One of our teachers was telling us a story, about the nice women in Argentina.

Ehsan: And how he was Casanova.

Adnan: How these girls were beautiful.

Ehsan: This is not acceptable.

On the other hand, trainee-teachers felt at ease learning with the Arab tutor due to the shared cultural and linguistic backgrounds:

Ehsan: We respect all teachers but Arabic one will be special for us…. He can understand us 100% and exactly. He knows our culture, our environment, everything.

Adnan: Not as other people who come from other culture. You have to explain and explain more to show your point.

Overall, the local cultural norms and religion had played a significant role in the adaptation of the offshore model in the context of Dubai and had an impact on trainee-teachers' learning. The tutors and trainee-teachers selectively negotiated the cultural implications of offshore education through their everyday curricular interactions.

Conclusion and implications of the study

This paper has described the way tutors and trainee-teachers engaged with a UK-derived offshore teacher education model in the context of Dubai. It has argued that the tutors and trainee-teachers as selective cosmopolitans negotiated the central tensions surrounding language and culture pragmatically and ambivalently in offshore education.

At a broader level, this study has shown that the business of adapting overseas education is not simply about moving education from one location to another, but about negotiating with local, cultural and religious belief systems in the context of the GCC region. This paper has sought to initiate discussion for understanding the much-neglected role of students and tutors in negotiating offshore education in local context. More importantly, it has sought to address a void in a modest way as there is almost nothing written about the impact of offshore education on people's identities in offshore education in the Middle East.

The findings have provided an insight into the consequence of globalisation on people's identities. Through our usage of the term 'selective cosmopolitans' we have described how individuals, in order to advantageously position themselves in the contemporary globalised world, negotiate between different cultural influences pragmatically, while simultaneously experiencing ambivalence and tensions in terms of their sense of identity. These individuals are inherently reflexive regarding the unavoidable complexity of their situation. This research set out by asking: 'Who is leading the process of internationalisation?' Based on this study, we contend that, in practice, neither the UK nor Dubai leads the process in Dubai's international education scene. The reality lies somewhere in the middle. It shows that people have a degree of agency in globalisation.

It is difficult to generalise the findings of this study for all programmes delivered offshore, for different kinds of programmes may follow different trajectories in different settings. While the English language and Western universities are likely to retain their significance in the foreseeable future, the very diversity of individuals and a vast supermarket of ideas and cosmopolitan experiences available to people mean that offshore education may take on different colours and contours in different contexts.

Note

1. The participants, many of whom are non-native speakers of English, have been quoted verbatim. All names are pseudonyms.

References

Altbach, P., and J. Knight. 2007. "The Internationalization of Higher Education: Motivations and Realities." *Journal of Studies in International Education* 11 (3–4): 290–305. doi:10.1177/1028315307303542.

Andrade, M. S. 2006. "International Students in English-Speaking Universities: Adjustment Factors." *Journal of Research in International Education* 5 (2): 131–154. doi:10.1177/1475240906065589.

Ballard, B., and J. Clanchy. 1997. *Teaching International Students*. Deakin: IDP Education Australia.

Beck, U. 2002. "The Cosmopolitan Perspective: Sociology of the Second Age of Modernity." *The British Journal of Sociology* 51 (1): 79–106.

Beck, U., and N. Sznaider. 2006. "Unpacking Cosmopolitanism for the Social Sciences: A Research Agenda." *The British Journal of Sociology* 57 (1): 1–23.

Böhm, A., M. Follari, A. Hewtt, S. Jones, N. Kemp, D. Meares, D. Pearce, and K. Van Cauter. 2004. *Vision 2020: Forecasting International Student Mobility: A UK Perspective.* London, UK: The British Council. http://www.britishcouncil.org/eumd_-_vision_2020.pdf

Briguglio, C., and R. Smith. 2012. "Perceptions of Chinese Students in an Australian University: Are We Meeting Their Needs?" *Asia Pacific Journal of Education* 32 (1): 17–33.

Brown, L. 2009. "An Ethnographic Study of the Friendship Patterns of International Students in England: An Attempt to Recreate Home through Conational Interaction." *International Journal of Educational Research* 48 (3): 184–193. doi: 10.1016/j.ijer.2009.07.003

Burden-Leahy, S. M. 2009. "Globalisation and Education in the Post-Colonial World: The Conundrum of the Higher Education System of the United Arab Emirates." *Comparative Education* 45 (4): 525–544. doi:10.1080/030 50060903391578.

Calhoun, C. 2006. *Cosmopolitanism and Belonging.* London: Routledge.

Cameron, D., and D. Block, eds. 2002. *Globalization and Language Teaching.* London: Routledge.

Centre for International Economics. 2008. Accessed September 30, 2009. http://www.thecie.com.au/

Chapman, A., and D. Pyvis. 2006a. "Dilemmas in the Formation of Student Identity in Offshore Higher Education: A Case Study in Hong Kong." *Educational Review* 58 (3): 291–302. doi:10.1080/00131910600748190.

Chapman, A., and D. Pyvis. 2006b. "Quality, Identity and Practice in Offshore University Programmes: Issues in the Internationalization of Australian Higher Education." *Teaching in Higher Education* 11 (2): 233–245. doi:10.1080/13562510500527818.

Conlon, G., A, Litchfield, and G., Sadlier. 2011. *Estimating the Value to the UK of Educational Exports.* BIS Research Paper No. 46. London: The Department for Business Innovation and Skills. Accessed September 30, 2009. http://www.bis.gov.uk/assets/biscore/higher-education/docs/e/11-980-estimating-value-of-education-exports.pdf

Connell, R. 2007. *Southern Theory: The Global Dynamics of Knowledge in Social Science.* Crows Nest, NSW: Allen and Unwin.

Crabtree, S. 2010. "Engaging Students from the United Arab Emirates in Culturally Responsive Education." *Innovations in Education and Teaching International* 47 (1): 85–94. doi:10.1080/14703290903525929.

Cronbach, L. J. 1971. "Test Validation." In *Educational Measurement*, 2nd ed., edited by R. L. Thorndike, 443–597. Washington, DC: American Council on Education.

Davis, D., A. Olsen, and A. Böhm. 2000. *Transnational Education. Providers, Partners and Policy: Challenges for Australian Institutions Offshore.* Brisbane: IDP Education Australia.

Debowski, S. 2003. *Lost in International Space: The Challenge of Academics Teaching Offshore.* Proceedings of the IDP Conference 'Securing the Future for International Education: Managing Growth and Diversity'. Melbourne: IDP Education Australia. Accessed August 8, 2007. http://www.idp.com/17aiecpapers/speakers/article344.asp

Delanty, G. 2006. "The Cosmopolitan Imagination: Critical Cosmopolitanism and Social Theory." *The British Journal of Sociology* 57 (1): 25–47. doi:10.1111/bjos.2006.57.issue-1.

Dobos, K. 2011. "Serving Two Masters" – Academics' Perspectives on Working at an Offshore Campus in Malaysia." *Educational Review* 63 (1): 19–35. doi:10.1080/00131911003748035.

Dubai International Academic City. 2013. "Company Profile." Accessed May 31, 2013. http://www.diacedu.ae/about-diac/company-profile

Dubai Statistics Centre. 2009. Accessed September 15, 2009. http://www.dubai.ae/en.portal?topic,SCDDEG,0,and_nfpb=trueand_pageLabel=dept

Dubai Strategic Plan 2015. Accessed June 15, 2009. http://www.dubai.ae/en.portal?topic,hm_dxbstgplan,0,and_nfpb=trueand_pageLabel=misc

Dunn, L., and M. Wallace. 2006. "Australian Academics and Transnational Teaching: An Exploratory Study of Their Preparedness and Experiences." *Higher Education Research and Development* 25 (4): 357–369.

Findlow, S. 2008. "Islam, Modernity and Education in the Arab States." *Intercultural Education* 19 (4): 337–352. doi:10.1080/14675980802376861.

Fine, R. 2006. *Cosmopolitanism*. London: Routledge.

Gainey, P., and C. Andressen. 2002. "The Japanese Education System: Globalisation and International Education." *Japanese Studies* 22 (2): 153–167. doi:10.1080/1037139022000016564.

Gardiner, H. 2006. "How Education Changes: Considerations of History, Science, and Values." In *Globalization: Culture and Education in the New Millennium*, edited by M. Suarez-Orozco and D. B. Qin-Hiliard, 235–258. Berkeley: University of California Press.

Giddens, A. 1999. *Runaway World: How Globalization is Reshaping Our Lives*. London: Profile.

Gribble, K., and C. Ziguras. 2003. "Learning to Teach Offshore: Pre-Departure Training for Lecturers in Transnational Programs." *Higher Education Research and Development* 22 (2): 205–216.

Hansen, D. T. 2008. "Curriculum and the Idea of a Cosmopolitan Inheritance." *Journal of Curriculum Studies* 40 (3): 289–312. doi:10.1080/0022027080 2036643.

Hayes, D., and R. Wynyard, eds. 2002. *The McDonaldisation of Higher Education*. New York: Praeger.

Heffernan, T., and D. Poole. 2005. "In Search of 'the Vibe': Creating Effective International Education Partnerships." *Higher Education* 50 (2): 223–246. doi:10.1007/s10734-004-6352-2.

Held, D. 2002. "Culture and Political Community: National, Global and Cosmopolitan." In *Conceiving Cosmopolitanism: Theory, Context and Practice*, edited by S. Vertovec and R. Cohen, 48–60. Oxford: Oxford University Press.

Higher Education Statistics Agency. 2009. Press Release 133. Accessed September 30, 2009. http://www.hesa.ac.uk/index.php/content/view/1398/161/

Huberman, M., and M. Miles. 2002. *The Qualitative Researcher's Companion*. Thousand Oaks, CA: Sage.

Jones, E. 2010. *Internationalisation and the Student Voice*. London: Routledge.

Kauppinen, I. 2012. "Towards Transnational Academic Capitalism." *Higher Education: The International Journal of Higher Education and Educational Planning* 64 (4): 543–556.

Kitzinger, J. 1995. "Qualitative Research: Introducing Focus Groups." *BMJ* 311 (7000): 299–302. doi:10.1136/bmj.311.7000.299.

Lane, J. E. 2011. "Importing Private Higher Education: International Branch Campuses." *Journal of Comparative Policy Analysis: Research and Practice* 13 (4): 367–381. doi:10.1080/13876988.2011.583106.

Leask, B., M. Hicks, M. Kohler, and B. King. 2005. *AVCC Offshore Quality Project: A Professional Development Framework for Academic Staff Teaching Australian Programs Offshore.* Adelaide: University of South Australia. Accessed May 24, 2009. http://www.aei.gov.au/AEI/GovernmentActivities/QAAustralian-EducationAndTrainingSystem/ USA_1_exSum_pdf.pdf

MacKinnon, D., and C. Manathunga. 2003. "Going Global with Assessment: What to Do When the Dominant Culture's Literacy Drives Assessment." *Higher Education Research and Development* 22 (2): 131–144.

Marginson, S., and G. Rhoades. 2002. "Beyond National States, Markets, and Systems of Higher Education: A Glonacal Agency Heuristic." *Higher Education* 43 (3): 281–309. doi:10.1023/A:1014699605875.

Massey, D. S., J. Arango, G. Hugo, A. Kouaouci, A. Pellegrino, and J. Edward Taylor. 1994. "An Evaluation of International Migration Theory: The North American Case." *Population and Development Review* 20 (4): 699–751. doi:10.2307/2137660.

McBurnie, G., and A. Pollock. 2000. "Opportunity and Risk in Transnational Education – Issues in Planning for International Campus Development: An Australian Perspective." *Higher Education in Europe* 25 (3): 333–343. doi:10.1080/713669272.

McBurnie, G., and C. Ziguras. 2007. *Transnational Education, Issues and Trends in Offshore Higher Education.* Abingdon: Routledge.

Miller-Idriss, C., and E. Hanauer. 2011. "Transnational Higher Education: Offshore Campuses in the Middle East." *Comparative Education* 47 (2): 181–207. doi:10.1080/03050068.2011.553935.

Mitsikopoulou, B. 2007. "The Interplay of the Global and the Local in English Language Learning and Electronic Communication Discourses and Practices in Greece." *Language and Education* 21 (3): 232–246. doi:10.2167/le749.0.

Ng, S. W. 2012. "Rethinking the Mission of Internationalization of Higher Education in the Asia-Pacific Region." *Compare: A Journal of Comparative and International Education* 42 (3): 439–459. doi:10.1080/03057925.2011.652815.

Noddings, N., ed. 2005. *Educating the Global Citizen.* New York: Teachers' College Press.

Nussbaum, M. 1997. *Cultivating Humanity: A Classical Defence of Reform in Liberal Education.* Cambridge, MA: Harvard University Press.

Oikonomidoy, E., and G. Williams. 2013. "Enriched or Latent Cosmopolitanism? Identity Negotiations of Female International Students from Japan in the US." *Discourse: Studies in the Cultural Politics of Education.* doi:10.1080/01596306.2012.71719.

Parry, R. 2007. *Re-coding the Museum: Digital Heritage and the Technologies of Change.* London and New York: Routledge.

Philips, T. 2002. "Imagined Communities and Self-Identity: An Exploratory Quantitative Analysis." *Sociology* 36 (3): 597–617. doi:10.1177/0038038502036003006.

Phillipson, R. 1992. *Linguistic Imperialism.* Oxford: Oxford University Press.

Poole, D., and C. Ewan. 2010. "Academics as Part-Time Marketers in University Offshore Programs: An Exploratory Study." *Journal of Higher Education Policy and Management* 32 (2): 149–158. doi:10.1080/13600800903575447.

Pratt, M. L. 1991. "Arts of the Contact Zone." Accessed September 30, 2009. http://www.class.uidaho.edu/thomas/English_506/Arts_of_the_Contact_Zone.pdf

Punch, K. A. 2005. *Introduction to Social Research: Quantitative and Qualitative Approaches*. 2nd ed. London: Sage.

Pyvis, D. 2007. "Why University Students Choose an International Education: A Case Study in Malaysia." *International Journal of Educational Development* 27 (2): 235–246. doi: 10.1016/j.ijedudev.2006.07.008.

Pyvis, D., and A. Chapman. 2007. "Why University Students Choose an International Education: A Case Study in Malaysia." *International Journal of Educational Development* 27 (2): 235–246.

Rizvi, F. 2005. "International Education and the Production of Cosmopolitan Identities." Accessed September 30, 2009. http://www.ideals.uiuc.edu/bitstream/handle/2142/3516/TSRizvi.pdf?sequence=2

Rizvi, F. 2010. "International Students and Doctoral Studies in Transnational Spaces." In *The Routledge Doctoral Supervisor's Companion: Supporting Effective Research in Education and the Social Sciences*, edited by M. Walker and P. Thomson, 158–170. London: Routledge.

Ryan, J. 2011. "Teaching and Learning for International Students: Towards a Transcultural Approach." *Teachers and Teaching* 17 (6): 631–648. doi:10.1080/13540602.2011.625138.

Sajitha, B. 2007. "Trends in International Trade in Higher Education: Implication and Options for Developing Countries." Education Working Paper Series, No. 6. Washington, DC: World Bank.

Schwandt, T. 2000. "Three Epistemological Stances for Qualitative Inquiry: Interpretivism, Hermeneutics and Social Constructionism." In *Handbook of Qualitative Research*, 2nd ed., edited by N. Denzin and Y. Lincoln, 189–213. Thousand Oaks, CA: Sage.

Schweisfurth, M., and Q. Gu. 2009. "Exploring the Experiences of International Students in UK Higher Education: Possibilities and Limits of Interculturality in University Life." *Intercultural Education* 20 (5): 463–473. doi:10.1080/14675980903371332.

Singh, P., and C. Doherty. 2004. "Global Cultural Flows and Pedagogic Dilemmas: Teaching in the Global University Contact Zone." *TESOL Quarterly* 38 (1): 9–42. doi:10.2307/3588257.

Skrbis, Z., and I. Woodward. 2007. "The Ambivalence of Ordinary Cosmopolitanism: Investigating the Limits of Cosmopolitan Openness." *The Sociological Review* 55 (4): 731–747.

Smith, L. 2009. "Sinking in the Sand? Academic Work in an Offshore Campus of an Australian University." *Higher Education Research & Development* 28 (5): 467–479.

Straw, W. 2011. "Globalisation: Reflecting on the Position and Future of UK Higher Education." Accessed September 30, 2009. http://www.guardian.co.uk/higher-education-network/blog/2011/oct/27/globalisation-policitc-uk-higher-education

Teichler, U. 2004. "The Changing Debate on Internationalisation of Higher Education." *Higher Education* 48 (1): 5–26. doi:10.1023/B:HIGH.0000033771.69078.41.

Urry, J. 2000. "The Global Media and Cosmopolitanism." Accessed September 1, 2009. http://www.lancs.ac.uk/fass/sociology/papers/urry-global-media.pdf

Urry, J. 2003. *Global Compexity*. Cambridge: Polity.

Vaish, V. 2008. "Mother Tongues, English, and Religion in Singapore." *World Englishes* 27 (3–4): 450–464. doi:10.1111/j.1467-971X.2008.00579.x.

Wang, T. 2007. "Understanding Chinese Educational Leaders' Conceptions in an International Education Context." *International Journal of Leadership in Education: Theory and Practice* 10 (1): 71–88. doi:10.1080/13603120500445275.

Waters, J., R. Brooks, and H. Pimlott-Wilson. 2011. "Youthful Escapes? British Students, Overseas Education and the Pursuit of Happiness." *Social & Cultural Geography* 12 (5): 455–469. doi:10.1080/14649365.2011.588802.

Weenink, D. 2008. "Cosmopolitanism as a Form of Capital: Parents Preparing Their Children for a Globalizing World." *Sociology* 42 (6): 1089–1106. doi:10.1177/0038038508096935.

Werbner, P. 1999. "Global Pathways: Working Class Cosmopolitans and the Creation of Transnational Ethnic Worlds." *Social Anthropology* 7 (1): 17–35. doi:10.1017/S0964028299000026.

Wilkins, S. 2001a. "Human Resource Development through Vocational Education in the United Arab Emirates: The Case of Dubai Polytechnic." *Journal of Vocational Education and Training* 54 (1): 5–26.

Wilkins, S. 2001b. "Student and Employer Perceptions of British Higher Education in the Arabian Gulf Region." *Research in Post-Compulsory Education* 6 (2): 157–174. doi:10.1080/13596740100200104.

Wilkins, S., M. S. Balakrishnan, and J. Huisman. 2012. "Student Satisfaction and Student Perceptions of Quality at International Branch Campuses in the United Arab Emirates." *Journal of Higher Education Policy and Management* 34 (5): 543–556. doi:10.1080/1360080X.2012.716003.

Ziguras, C. 1999. "Cultural Diversity and Transnational Flexible Delivery." Paper presented at the 16th Annual Conference of the Australasian Society for Computers in Learning in Tertiary Education, Brisbane, December 5–8.

Index

INDEX